Apple

Skin to the Core

ALSO BY ERIC GANSWORTH

Novels:

Indian Summers*

Smoke Dancing*

Mending Skins*

Extra Indians*

If I Ever Get Out of Here*

Give Me Some Truth*

Poetry Collections:

Nickel Eclipse: Iroquois Moon*

A Half-Life of Cardio-Pulmonary Function*

From the Western Door to the Lower West Side

(collaboration with photographer Milton Rogovin)

Creative Non-Fiction, poems:

Breathing the Monster Alive*

Drama:

Re-Creation Story*

Rabbit Dance*

Home Fires and Reservation Roads*

Patriot Act

Editor:

Sovereign Bones: New Native American Writing, Volume II

*includes visual art by the author

A MEMOIR
in Words and Pictures

Eric Gansworth

LQ

LEVINE QUERIDO

MONTCLAIR · AMSTERDAM · NEW YORK

This is an Arthur A. Levine book
Published by Levine Querido

www.levinequerido.com • info@levinequerido.com
Levine Querido is distributed by Chronicle Books LLC

Library of Congress Control Number: 2019957000
ISBN 978-1-64614-013-8
Printed and bound in China

Published October 2020
Fourth Printing

for the Bumblebee,
pollinating apples, and so much more,

for the apples embracing their skins,
and the Skins embracing they're Apples.

CONTENTS

DOG STREET

Side A

Come Together
Something
Maxwell's Silver Hammer
Oh! Darling
Octopus's Garden
I Want You (She's So Heavy)

Side B

Here Comes the Sun
Because
You Never Give Me Your Money
Sun King
Mean Mr. Mustard
Polythene Pam
She Came in Through the Bathroom Window
Golden Slumbers
Carry That Weight
The End

Her Majesty

GET BACK

Peel This Skin
Indian Love Call
Are These Tricks or Are These Treats?
Legacy
Everybody Knows
Poem to the Beams in My Uncle's House, Empty These Days
My Mother Delivers a Quick Lesson in Survival and History

LINER NOTES

APPLE RECORDS

We say we want a revolution,
well, we know, you all want to change
the world.

We tell you that it's evolution,
well, we know, you all want to change
the world,

but when we talk about reconstruction,
don't I know that I can count you out.

Uncle Tomahawk Hangs Around the Fort Until He Finds His Own Metaphor

Some Indians feel that to spend too much time
among white people is to risk losing everything
we call our own, even though that idea is itself
loosely defined. Sometimes, we borrow from
other Indians and sometimes, like that ten dollars
we asked for when we were desperate, we forget
what we've borrowed until we are reminded.

Socials and Powwows bring us together, because
they celebrate all the ways we maintain our own
ways of life. We know the dances and the songs,
the exact rhythm patterns for drums and rattles.

But we've borrowed dances from other nations. We have
no alligators in the Northeast, no real-world example to borrow
in creating these moves, and yet, Alligator Dance has
been with us for so long, it feels like ours, free and clear.

Even our singers who know the songs best have lost
the words to some, reduced to memorizing sound.
When patterns and syllables are all you have, you go
with them, and pass them down to the next group of young
people willing to sit and learn beside you on the Social
bench, knowing they'll just be rough, knowing they're going
to misstep on the floor where we dance. This is no game.
But even as we keep our own sounds and borrow
from other Indians, we sometimes snag our metaphors
from others and our relationships to them until we find
the right ones to call our own, and memorize them.

As a reminder of what we risk, spending too much time
with white people, some Indians first come up with Uncle
Tomahawk. Even Indians who have never read Harriet Beecher
Stowe, or who couldn't give you any details about Uncle
Tom as a character, know what the name means, how
the Tomahawk will always signal "Indian," how the "Uncle"
is never a true relative here. We pride ourselves on being
clever with originality and we know that Uncle Tom is already
a knife-sharp slur for the same behavior within a different group.
They have their own history of being tortured and killed by white
people, their own struggles with the nuances of the individual life.

Some Indians next come up with Hang-Around-the-Fort Indian.
The fort was designed to give white people shelter and sustenance
when they needed a break from "taming the West" by killing Indians
directly or wiping out the original food sources, so Indians would starve
on their own without the fort's residents bloodying their own hands.
But it was a name born of stories involving real Indians, hanging
around with real white soldiers, hoping to find secrets to surviving
the onslaught, braving direct contact while others waited and starved.

While we could laugh about weapons and forts, no one invoked Carlisle,
Hampton, and all the ways the boarding schools changed us forever. No
metaphors encompass our wiped memories and families, skins intact because
no bleach would make us white enough to disappear entirely. But one day, some Indian
finally bit an apple, exposed the blinding white flesh inside, contrast vibrating
against broken red skin. Like Sir Isaac Newton, after insight hit in falling fruit,
they recognized the perfect label for Indians not sharp enough to make it all the way
home, left in that space between two places. *Red on the outside, white on the inside,*
forever locked away from both worlds, separated by the thinnest membrane.

Boarding School Philosophy, Shorter, Simplified Edition: Practical Application

Problem: Indians in communities will reproduce
                in both form and idea. If offspring cannot be stopped, disrupt culture.
Solution 1:   Kill them all, or remove all available food sources.
Solution 2:   Destabilize group identity by making group land base illegal.
Solution 3:   Where land base exists, sterilize fertile adults under the guise of current
                helpful medical care, until they vanish on their own, unaware.
Solution 4:   Remove present juvenile offspring, incarcerate them long enough
                to open possibilities for future manual labor resources. To minimize
                bloodshed, call incarceration institution a "school," convince
                parents this is an Opportunity of a Lifetime for juvenile offspring.

                If students attempt to return
                        (and they will)
                and attempt to procreate with their own kind
                        (and they will)
                the remnants of their culture will be so small,
                so fragmented, they will have no choice but to build
                new lives drawn from the available current American
                cultural resources.

Optimally, within two generations, those slivers of their old cultures
will be so small, they cannot thrive, and assimilation will be complete.

Uncontrollable Variables:
                those who decline the opportunity of incarceration
                the presence of mirrors and the capacity for insight.
Long-Range Plan: Repeat as necessary. Revisit in two generations' time. Adjust
accordingly.

Hello, My Name Is . . .

1.

It begins with your great-grandparents. Having five
children, Leander, Orsamus, Howard, Alberta, Willard,
they wonder how they will divide the reservation land
in their name among them, if all five can make it as farmers.
That profession seems like their only prospect in Niagara County,
at the beginning of the twentieth century, where the reservation
and the settlements surrounding it do not mix much, worlds
immeasurably far apart from each other despite the minimal miles.

One day, a man shows up with the Opportunity of a Life
Time, he says, offering an introduction to that world beyond
the borders, should they need it at some time. (As an aside,
he assures them their children *will* need it.) The school
would cost the family nothing and the children would learn,
in a military-style environment, useful trades and insider secrets
of American life not available within the reservation's confines.

Wanting to give all of their children that opportunity, they
agree to send them to Carlisle, Pennsylvania, three hundred
miles away. The school, understanding the hardship of travel,
offers a Summer Outing program, so the children do not have
to come home. If they are *good enough*, they will be placed
with white families, working off their board as labor, all
the while learning that paler life, day in and day out.

They do not seem to understand that the only life learned
will be how to work for white people, expenses deducted
from their pay for the room they sleep in after work, food
they eat at these houses while indentured for summer
months between the school years for five calendar years.

Five years was the optimal amount of time school officials
believed it would take for children to find it impossible to rejoin
their old lives. Five years away would assure their discomfort
in the places they'd left, offering them one option: to try to assimilate.
              (this was not included in the sales pitch for "free education")

The school, founded by a military man,
Richard Henry Pratt, had an explicit mission:
"Kill the Indian! Save the Man." Pratt so delighted
in proclaiming this anywhere else he spoke
of the place, he never noticed that his
proudest achievement began with the word "Kill"
              (it can be safely assumed that the school representative
              also failed to include this philosophy in the pitch).

You might ask: what Indian parents would allow their children
out the door and across the border, with strangers, destined
to arrive at a place whose sole purpose was to strip them
of everything they had been, a place designed to kill the only
culture they knew, and replace it with something else?

Of the five children, two never returned to their home
territories, one arrived near home, staying on the periphery,
living out his life thirty miles away, and two came back
and reacquainted themselves with the lives they had
almost lost, marrying young women from home,
starting families, and keeping our name going forward.

I wondered how, of the five, my grandfather was one
of the two who successfully came back home, and I am
nosy enough to ask people until I find the answer.
Carlisle, an abandoned military barracks, from the beginning

had been the perfect breeding ground for infectious diseases.
Indian children were dormed, four beds to each cramped room
and for hundreds of early students, the last room they ever lived in.

Exposed to diseases from England and Europe, in
a few short bursts (a staff member sneeze, a cough, droplets
spreading in those tiny four-person rooms), these students
became bodies that had never been exposed, and caught
tuberculosis. They learned all the ravages it could cause
inside those walls. They learned they were allowed
to die there, and they learned to be buried in unmarked
mass graves near the school, sometimes dismembered
and dissected in the name of western medicine. They learned
to become nameless skeletons who, even now, linger in dusty
drawers of libraries and museums in eastern Pennsylvania,
not afforded the liberty celebrated in the cracked bell
a short distance away, their current custodians not wanting
to admit their part in keeping these bones from their home
lands, even if that part just means keeping their own mouths shut.

The motto, "Kill the Indian, Kill the Man," was maybe close
enough for Pratt and his school. You wonder how long
this practice would have continued had those parents not
come looking for their children who'd stopped writing
them monthly letters, from their promised New World
Place, New World Life, New World Chance for Survival.

By the time my grandfather arrived at Carlisle, those
unmarked graves were filled to capacity. When he began
coughing, he was sent back to the reservation to recuperate,
with assurances he could resume his education, if and when
he recovered from the disease his education had exposed
him to, infecting him with the Old World in his New World.

Off and on, he went and returned, continuing
to grow ill, then recovering at home, heading
back to school with his siblings, models of success.
As he built up his resistance to new diseases, he also
developed resistance to walking away from the world
where his roots lay, growing deeper and tougher with each
trip back to the homestead where his parents worried about
their children who left, and their children who returned.
His repeated visits back allowed him to build up immunities
to the school itself, and follow his desire to come home and start a family.

2.

My grandfather died so many years before I was
born, his life is a collection of stories people told
over our dining room table. In my life I've seen three
fleeting images, some now stored only in my memory.
The first photo was lost when our family home exploded
in a ridiculous accident decades later, where almost everything
we'd accumulated for over a hundred years went up in a thirty-
minute inferno, including the one photo of him, as a small child,
barely able to keep his balance. He has very long hair past
his shoulder blades, and if the photo had not been a sepia tintype,
if he had not been wearing a traditional ribbon shirt, I would swear
the baby in the photo was my brother, learning to walk, gripping
a chair leg to steady himself as his journey begins, one step at a time.

The second photo is my grandfather at Carlisle, revealing nothing
more to the photographer than his new identity, nothing more than
he had to. When children arrived at the school, they discovered
their packed bags irrelevant. Their hair was cut, traditional
clothes swapped for military uniforms, moccasins for boots.
They had no way of knowing, climbing on those trains to Carlisle,

or Hampton, or Haskell, or any of the other 397 schools, that
even before those scissors came out, many had to check
their identities and anything that made them Indians
at the gate, like overcoats their host considered a hindrance.

If your name was too traditional, you were forced
to choose a new one from a list of acceptable American
names, wall-mounted in the room where they were
inducted, their first forced act in becoming someone else.
After you had been wiped clean of the only name
you'd ever known, next came your clothes and your
hair, your language, then your religion, your way of
understanding the world, your culture, your self.

Richard Henry Pratt never had to leave his name
behind, become a person he'd never met, never heard
of. He believed in what he was doing, so proud of his
slogan and the "progress" it represented, like an advertising
jingle you can't get out of your head. He believed this
was progress because all of the other white men in
the U.S. Military at the time wanted to stop after
the first phrase. Pratt understood there was only one way
to deal with his greatest fear, that his charges would
"go back to the blanket," and he used that fear to shape
his mission, one tattered military blanket at a time.

Lucky for us, we had one white ancestor, who gave
us our last name, in 17-something, marrying our great-
great-great-great-great-great-great-grandmother, bridging
two cultures in one intimate location, running from
the rules of his aristocratic family, running to discover
life on the wild side. Equally lucky, a reservation school

teacher thought Gansevoort was too exotic and changed
our names and our lives, forever, with a quick scrawl
from her quill pen. She Americanized our name until we
suited her taste, like real, breathing ingredients in her
melting pot, so my grandfather got to keep at least his
name intact when he came back and resumed his life
on the reservation, as so few other students did.

Though he did not stay at Carlisle as long as his brothers and sister,
the last photo I've seen of my grandfather hints that the place lingered
in his soul. He is an adult, short like me, standing with other members
of the Tuscarora community in a group shot, early adopters of basketball,
in 1920. By then, Carlisle had been shut down, its mission recognized
for the genocidal practice, cultural and physical, at its heart. But
the photo suggests he is not taking his chances. Most in the group wear
uniforms of the sport, running shoes, long socks, shorts, tank tops.
Flanking them, he is fully dressed in a three-piece suit, leather shoes
shined, and necktie in a perfect Windsor knot. Even here, he seems
to fear revealing a wild side, fear the possibility that government
agents will return to his door, demand he gather his things,
forcing him to get back on the train to Carlisle for remediation.

3.

Here is what little else I know, reading records, remembering
the slivers my grandmother would speak, when she thought
it was safe to do so, all those years later:

> Your job at the school was to start over, be a blank
> slate and, because you are a child at the time, it never
> occurs to you that white children are not stripped
> of their culture and punished for speaking the only
> language they know. It never occurs to you that

you are not being taught how to be an American
but how to lose yourself. It never occurs to you
(because you can't imagine yet having children
of your own) that you are being taught systematically
to forget so that you will have nothing left to pass
on to your children when they arrive. You are not being
taught how to adapt and survive in America.
You are being wiped clean so that whatever reservoir
of information you retain, will only reference a certain
version of American culture, the melting pot that does not
melt, and when you open your mouth, to teach your children
what you know, you discover there is no blanket to go back
to. It has been pulled away from you, one thread at a time,
unraveled as you worked in stables, and shops, as farmhands
and domestics, until what you hold in your hand is not
even enough thread to tie your hair back. It doesn't matter,
as your hair is no longer a length that needs restraining.

4.

I am not one of the thousands of Indians around the country
who were led away into one of 400 boarding schools on
a promise that they would learn to survive. This is not my
direct experience. This is not my parents' experience directly,
but we are close enough. I am only two generations removed
from that attempt to remove us and make us disappear.

Pratt tried to keep my grandparents at Carlisle long enough
to drain that reservoir, but they made it back with memories
intact. And two generations later, we continue to find those
fragments, pick up pieces and situate them back in the puzzle
frame. We hope we can figure out what all the missing pieces
should look like, so we can rebuild them from scratch.

There are fewer of us on the reservation than it seems
there should be, if you compare us to the other families.

But other Gansworths live on, knowing
nothing of us, in Philadelphia and Davenport,
Iowa, places my grandfather's brothers landed,
knowing they had stayed too long at Carlisle,
erasing themselves too fully to ever come home.

5.

Of the three siblings who could get back, one brother lived in Buffalo,
thirty miles south, after graduating from Princeton. I have seen photos
of him in his dorm room, and in later shots, he stands in shirtsleeves
with family in a reservation "homestead" garden before putting on
his suit jacket and heading to his own home, where he and his wife
lived out their days, having chosen to have no children.

The second brother married, and had a single daughter,
spending the rest of his life at the reservation's northern
border, overlooking Lewiston and across Lake Ontario,
Toronto glimpsed on the occasional clear day, maybe
assured that he could absolutely care for one child.

My grandfather and grandmother, marrying in the City
of Brotherly Love, made their way home, the fears and
questions their parents had about which children would live
at the homestead, answered. Like his two close brothers,
my grandfather stayed disciplined, minding the number
of children he and his wife would bring into the world,
minding the names they gave those children, all drawn
from family history, some gone, but not forgotten.

They raised their three children—my uncle, my aunt, my father—
on that same plot of land where the government agent had

stepped through the threshold, promising great opportunities
for the future. I wonder, as I study every entry I can find,
how diligently they guarded the door, for the rest of their lives,
giving their children the materials to reweave our story, each
broken thread mended and tightened until they made a blanket
to wrap around themselves, share their warmth until the storm passes.

6.

And if this seems confusing, tracing all these generations
and keeping the shattered pieces of their stories straight,
imagine how we do it, retelling ourselves the details over
and over, committing them to memory, filling in
the missing fragments as we find them, along the way.

And if this seems confusing, tracing all these
generations and keeping shattered pieces of their
stories straight, imagine why we do it, so that no
one can show back up, with an Opportunity of a Life
Time, to give us a new life, to help us disappear
when our backs are turned, when we aren't looking.

7.

There are recordings of my grandmother, made in the middle
of the twentieth century, before I am born. She is speaking to us
from the Spirit World, with the aid of an Ethnographer and
a primitive mid-century microphone, a crude electronic Ouija
Board humming in warming tubes and resistors, using mostly
the Tuscarora language occasionally cut with her newer English.

Around this same time, she resurrects a talent that lay
dormant from her childhood, that stretches back so far,
it begins in the time when men were hunters and women
were responsible for a family's agricultural life, growing
plants and saving seeds for the next year's harvest.

She makes cornhusk dolls, dressing them in clothing
she makes from scraps left over from clothes she has
made for herself, her family. These dolls, she sends into
the world, to support herself, her family, sold to interested
outsiders at events celebrating our culture. But because they are
designed for an audience beyond our world, she accommodates.

When men were hunters, gone for long stretches,
they carried dolls with them to represent each member
of their families left behind, to keep them company
on the lonely task of providing for them a future.
Women who made them traditionally did not include
faces. Some people say this was a part of the doll's origin
story, a hedge against vanity, if you have too lovely
a face. Others whisper that a doll with a face might invite
a wandering spirit to take up residence behind those features.

Either way, when a newspaper reporter composes a feature
on my grandmother's creations, the dolls she shows in
the accompanying photo have small dots and straight lines,
arranged purposefully into faces on the dried husks, mathematical
notations she was taught at Carlisle, two decimal points,
the symbol for subtraction. She displays these faces, revealing
her own tentative smile for the news, for the world, to show
she did not harbor quaint ideas about the unseen world. But maybe,
the whole time, she is thinking about all the wandering spirits
of children who did not survive Carlisle, who did not make it
home. Maybe she is inviting them into a place not quite the same
as the reservation they left, but maybe close enough for now.

My grandmother understands the risks involved in
her image being recorded, as proof of something not
of her making, but she also maybe understands posterity,

that opportunity for a better future could be true, this time, and she chooses to imagine us and our futures decades before we come into being, to carry our name forward with the tools and dreams we have available to us.

Naming Ceremony

1.

Should you be an enrolled member of your nation, and should your family choose, and have the opportunity, you may go through ceremony, and be given the name the Creator will know you by, for the rest of your life. It is a part of you and no one else will have it while you walk the Earth. You do not do this lightly, or casually, and sometimes, you are the person who waits a very very long time, and you will be reminded when the time comes, that you have chosen to wait a very very long time, if you see it through.

2.

Because naming is a part of your life, casual informal versions of this ritual crop up. You will be given nicknames that do not necessarily carry an effect you've desired. The ability to laugh at yourself is more common as a ceremony. For this one, you do not need to set aside days to participate in formal community ceremonies that come along only a couple times a year.

Some names come from your quirks you will never get used to knowing. They are the secret language of people who love you. You will wonder, when you hear your harsh nickname, for the five thousandth time, how people who love you can saddle you with something that feels more like an ever-fresh scab, a wound ripped open over and over, before it can even have a chance to heal over, flake off, leave a scar.

Other nicknames exhibit the force of will. Your parents name you after nine months of laboring over the right sound, the right look, because English, even if it is our first language now, is still our second language. And then, when you are an infant, your siblings, or your uncle or auntie or cousins, decide you will have a different name, entirely, sometimes not a name at all, just a sound instead, a series of syllables that, within months, will seem totally natural to everyone.

Even your parents with their other intentions, end up using your legal name only as a threat, warning you that you are testing their patience. It might be listed in the birth records of the United States, New York State, Niagara County, a different place beyond the borders of your homeland, but only your bad behavior is enough to awaken your Christian name in the mouths of your parents, at the end of their wits.

3.

You may even discover that a name given in innocence can turn on you. Among the dozen or so names I've been given over my lifetime, most have atrophied in misuse or fallen to obscurity. The people who used them have grown up with me, and we are all different people now, and they might resurrect one for an occasional laugh but the names have not retained the longevity of two that have survived into my current life.

It is easy to see why I'd be okay with Batman. Though it does have sociopathic connotations, the idea of being a vigilante hero with an awesome car still holds all the appeal it ever did.

But Pixie Dust has decided drawbacks as a name. Even the existence of a hard-rocking, genre-defining, ear-bleeding rock band can't remove the fey daintiness of the name my brother randomly gave me after we watched an episode of *Gumby* together as kids. Within it, Gumby and Pokey jump into a fairy tale, concerning a clueless prince and the girl he wants to marry. He is bamboozled by unethical merchants, but before he can deliver the lame gift he plans to offer his love, he selflessly helps an elf, who returns the kind gesture, transforming his gift of real tree and a real pigeon into golden replicas, with his bag of magic Pixie Dust. What this story has to do with me, I have no idea, but my brother decided I should immediately be renamed Pixie Dust or if you are more into brevity, Pixie for short.

What might be cute when you are five or six, has distinct drawbacks when you are sixteen, trying to compete in an aggressive Shirts and Skins game of backyard basketball with your cousins who play as if it were a blood sport (which it always is with them), or deciding who gets to choose the next album to play, when we stick the speakers out the window and share our loves.

Your passion for David Bowie, Blondie, Queen, the B-52's, and the Go-Go's affirms your essential Pixie-ness to your Lynyrd Skynyrd, Molly Hatchet, ZZ Top, and Deep Purple–loving cousins. Even your devotion to the Beatles is scorned by their devotion to the Stones in that debate over taste and testosterone on the Rez where those distinctions are front and center.

4.

You can never give yourself a nickname. If you try, you will be doomed in the most subtle of ways. People will call you by that desired name, with the slightest inflection of laughter and pity. If we try to conjure our own nicknames, we reveal our vanity, our secret desires. Sometimes you are lucky and you grow out of a nickname and then back into it fully with just a few short years of embarrassment, then resignation, acceptance, and joy.

If you are from somewhere else (and sometimes even if you are from the Rez, and have spent your whole life there), you may wonder about the harshness. Even some of the most sharp-tongued, cleverest people who come up with the nicknames that stay like scar tissue may not know how they inherited such a talent.

5.

But inside, at the core, we understand this is preparation. When you live in a community on a landmass five miles by seven miles, you will spend many hours working beyond those borders, shopping beyond those borders, eating in restaurants beyond those borders, breathing the air beyond those borders. Every time you leave that home sign behind, even for a little while, you are likely to hear, in some form or another, that those surrounding you view you as *Lesser*.

If you excel, you will be "remarkable for being an Indian."
If you fail, you will be "no surprise because you're an Indian."

Every observation in between extremes will be framed, even compliments given in surprise and disbelief, and little more.

When you live with a nickname, you are more prepared for whatever unexpected beliefs are tossed your way, casually, or said within earshot because you do or do not fit someone else's idea of what an Indian is. And when you are frustrated and wonder why people who are connected to you for your lifetime would do this to you, you remember.

6.

You remember that they have been here before, they have heard everything you're going to hear. They have their own wounds that won't heal into scabs and then scars, but because they, like you, are grandchildren of Boarding School survivors, they know you need to be tough and sensitive. They know you can't let the calluses get so deadened to feeling that you forget how close you were to disappearing altogether.

7.

You have heard the harshest of all nicknames, the one that insists Pratt had worked his Boarding School magic/voodoo on your family and that you carry that Apple curse at your core, embedded in the little brown teardrop-shaped seeds that rest there, like auricles and ventricles of the heart. You wonder who came up with this nickname, who bit into an apple first, looked at it, crisp cold skin and flesh in their mouth, juice sliding down their dark chin.

8.

If your nickname harbors especially sharp contours, like a shattered mirror, everyone you know will claim to have invented it. Because our verbal talents allowed us to survive, even when we were supposed to burn our cultures out like self-cleaning ovens, we prize cleverness, quickness, the ability to find the right metaphor to reveal and obscure at the exact same time, depending on whose ears are receiving our words in the moment.

All kinds of people on the Rez will line up to claim their grandmother or grandfather did this or that, invented that or this beadwork pattern. But no one says they have a Cherokee Princess Great-Great-Grandmother, and no one says "look at my cheekbones, look at my cheekbones." No one is spitting into test tubes and shipping their saliva off to *23andMyAncestralSpiritAnimal.com*. No one needs to claim a little exotic blood coursing through their suburban lives, hoping to fill their two-car garages with it, like that elevator in *The Shining*, flooding the lobby and everything.

And no one claims to be the First Indian to call another Indian an Apple. I have never heard of anyone claiming their relatives came up with the idea, claiming that one of their own had picked up the shattered mirror, daring to risk its edges, discovering the flesh hidden inside.

9.

After all this time, and all these attempts to wipe us out, some things are on the verge of disappearing, some things are gone. Our stories survive in wampum belts, woven rows of purple shell beads and white, in sequence and arrangement, revealing an image in the contrast between the colors, that documents our history, cosmology, culture.

Without living people to commit the stories to memory, those belts become merely shapes, vague images. I have seen wampum belts whose original meaning is lost. The last person who knew how to read them left the Earth, returned to the Skyworld without passing its story along for us.

Did that person choose silence, or was no one paying attention, the last time that story was told?

The wampum belts remain, but without memory, they tell a different story. They show us everything we have lost, everything we can still save, by telling and retelling the stories we know, the stories of our lives.

10.

A primary lesson we are taught, even in our greatest sadness: we must clear our eyes, our ears, our throats to do our parts in carrying on the stories for the time we will no longer be able to pass them on, leaving silent images behind, mere mysteries to others. This is our foundation.

11.

I tell you here what I have seen, what I have heard, what I have lived. I choose not to be silent, and you can choose to open your ears, and eyes, or close them. Maybe this story is not for you. We can agree that we each see the world differently, and each have a contribution to the larger story, and believe we have things to learn from each other.

My Grandmothers Gain Nicknames by Relative Proximity

My two grandmothers have both encountered the world
of boarding schools, Carlisle and Hampton. Both speak
fluent Tuscarora to friends; they use only English with
their children. They insist their children regularly attend
local schools, to avoid putting them on the trains.

Carlisle is gone, but some boarding schools
still exist farther west, and you never know
when a government agent might show
at your door and tell you of a lucky break
for your children, or accuse you of neglect
so they will be justified in taking them away
for an unspecified time they deem is right.

When they become grandmothers, these two look
to separate themselves. One is robust and the other,
smaller, so they easily adopt Big and Little. They both
refuse to be called Gooo-soood. They don't want
Tuscarora to leak into the brains and vocabularies
of the next generation, landing instead on "Oma,"
the word used in the German Settlements surrounding
the Rez, inventing their own spelling to keep separate.

I wonder if they ever forgot their old names,
earlier lives, as they become Little Umma,
my father's mother, and Big Umma, my mother's.
My mom's father becomes Umps, in complement to
his wife, but because my father's father has walked
on before he became a grandfather, he remains

"Willard" to us, the boy too sickly to stay at Carlisle,
giving himself a chance to come home.

Sometimes one small act of subversion is enough
to save a story, a history, a line of newer generations
who will sift through fragments and rebuild the story
from scratch. Did he imagine we would reach for
memories and metaphors to shore up the places
where stories have been silenced, where names have
become indistinct, swapped for something more
acceptable, undetectable to those around them?

As he coughed and coughed, did he dream one day we
would arrive and rescue his memory, his name from that
place in eastern Pennsylvania and keep it here, safe and sound?

Little Umma Reads the Ethnographer's Rorschach Cards

I imagine Big Umma would refuse to talk with him,
when he comes to live on the Rez for a period
in someone's upstairs. She was adventurous enough
to have dressed in her finest, a fresh crocheted collar
for her good black dress, and visited New York City
with Umps, to see for herself if the tall buildings Indian
men worked on really did scrape the sky like people said,
and if they did, what was visible on the other side. She did
not believe in Skywoman, Skyworld, or the dome between
that place and this one, though she firmly committed to Heaven
and Hell, sin and salvation. But Big Umma was Onondaga and used
to going it alone; she was okay as an outsider among outsiders.

Little Umma was Tuscarora, perhaps prone to greater
peer pressure within her community. So when
it becomes a minor fad to visit the squatting
ethnographer and answer his questions about
the series of inkblot shapes he shows everyone,
she willingly makes arrangements for her turn.

We frustrate the ethnographer because we refuse to meet
with him alone to respond to his inkblots, always demanding
a witness group of our peers. He admits defeat, telling himself
this is group behavior in a group rebuilding itself after
multiple attempts at disruption. Maybe he is right, but maybe
we fear he will try something untoward, if any of us is alone
with him in his room, with no one around to see what he does
and doesn't do. Some memories die harder than others and he
seems oblivious to this possibility, and flips through the cards.

He feels people are talking about the right
answers, though he assures them there are
no right answers.

        (but of course, we know there are)

The cards are the standard set, and he is trying
to determine if their answers match the answers
of white people. How does he not know, living
here as he does, that even if we see a wolf,
that we see a Wolf, one of our clans, and that
it is not merely a wild cousin of the dog, a villain
in multiple fairy tales and metaphors, that Wolf
binds us together instead of tearing us apart?

He later regrets having performed these tests
because they will potentially be used by officials
to argue that we are of inferior intelligence, and so
he has had the records sealed until so far away
a date that I will be long dead before that day.

I will never know if Little Umma sees two
women in fancy bustle dresses flanking
a tree, picking fruit from the ground. I will
never know if the fruit she imagines
is an apple. The reservation has plenty
of orchards and she attends the Baptist
Church, so she's familiar with the power
of apples, real and metaphoric.

She is still alive when Apple transubstantiates for Indians
into an accusation that might be pointed at her, but she is
working her way toward living a century at the time,

and sees fewer people, and hears less of what is spoken to her.
She is safe with her Biblical and Agricultural Apples.
Though she survives the Boarding School and the Outings
Program, she will never be confronted about things that were
out of her control when her parents put her on that train,
particularly if spoken by younger Indians who were never
forced to experience either of those transformations.

Those Indians whose parents refused to send them
to the schools had time to develop their own metaphors,
their own nicknames, hot as cauterized flesh, reminding Pratt
            (as if he could hear them)
that not even he could strip Indians of their skin, the features
they would carry around every day for the rest of their lives.
Only other Indians could crack that skin, make it
less valuable, and only those survivors who made it
back could dismiss the idea. Only those survivors
understood that an Apple, once its red skin was split,
would brown back on the inside, exposed to the light
and air of the family's histories and bones.

Big Umma Delivers a Quick Lesson in History and Survival

In nearly every reservation home except ours, I see the carousel
housing little containers of beads, often grouped according
to color, a card with sewing needles of different sizes, scraps
of cloth and leather, paper for patterns, pincushions, and scissors.
We have a sewing basket, and my mother makes neat repairs and
remounts missing buttons while watching *Jeopardy!* and *Wheel of
Fortune*, never sticking herself even keeping her eyes mostly on the TV.

I ask her once why she never does beadwork, never even keeps
materials around for the possibility. She gets up and finds
with no effort, in her piles of assorted belongings, a coffee
can drum I made in elementary school. I'd decorated the can
with construction paper, to hide its Hills Bros. skin, run rawhide
straps through the two pieces of tanned hide, tying them tight,
finally drawing "Indian symbols" in Magic Marker on the taut
hide head, the place you would strike it to make the right sound.

She says that would have never happened when she was in school.
She brought home beadwork once, beadwork the new Rez elementary
school teacher had taught her class to do. Big Umma took it back and told
the teacher if she'd wanted her children to learn backwards skills, she
would have kept them useful at home to work gardens instead
of sending them to school, where they could learn to be different
people. The ghost of Pratt whispered lessons to her all the time.
My mother could play the piano and sing harmony, but in her
younger years, learned only hymns in service of the Baptist Church
Umps and Umma attended, to the point where the only Socials
she knew, were those held after Sunday School, in service of the Lord.

THE RED ALBUM

We Were Only Waiting
for This Moment
to Arrive

A Note to Those Who Know My Family

If you're just that kind who loves Eee-ogg
or just that kind who loves taking your Big Spoon
and stirring the pot, you can close
the gaping jaws you're getting ready
to rattle in the direction of my family
and put your spoon back in whatever
handy drawer it came out of.

      We've had the conversation already
      and they fully know this is the story
      of my memories and that memories are
      like those little pieces of plastic spinning
      in the snow globes, some opaque and some
      gleaming like the edges of broken glass,
      shifting and ever changing, never quite
      the exact pattern you might hope for, like
      the kind of snow globe souvenir you can buy
      in the shops down at the falls, near the place
      where people from our community sell beadwork
      and jewelry, little jitterbug people, picture
      frames and pincushions, offering their own
      touchstones of our stories, our memories for others.

      I'm not claiming to know anyone else's story
      well enough to tell it. This is my own. We are
      Onondagas who have been with Tuscaroras
      since the beginning, a string of memory from one
      part of the confederacy to another. But because
      that is true, we are always a little bit outside
      of either place, connected and not tethered

at the same time. This state is bound to lead
to something getting lost in translation. As
flawed as it is, this is my understanding of how
I came to be where I am now, documenting
what I still remember and what I have been told
by people I can no longer ask because their voices
are gone for good. As a young person, I looked
for a long time to find a story like mine in books
I read, and tired of not finding it, I decided to write
my own and hope I might also be doing someone
else a favor along the way. If you pick this up,
and it seems familiar to you, then you'll know
what I believe about the value of our memories,
the value of our lives measured against any other.

If you are looking for yourself, to see if there is any story
with Eee-ogg at its heart, I suggest your mirror is a more
productive place to find what you're looking for.

We keep snapshots, frozen seconds of life, loosely
organized in the Red Album engraved with *Memories*
on its fake leather cover. This collection is a map
to survival, a fragmented history of a time already
fading from the upper mountain, over to Dog Street
and a trip through the swamp, a messy celebration,
with unexpected turns, some dead ends, and a love song
to eternal mystery housed in a universe five miles by
seven miles, a universe we each know, but in our own ways.

How Dog Street Gets Its Name

Most Rez Roads are named for families
who lived there first, or had the most kids
spreading across their patch of land.
Two are named for outside routes they
follow, leading you beyond the territories
from the south, northeast, and northwest.

On any map, the road dividing the Rez right
down the middle is listed as Mount Hope. I
guess the cartographer had a sense of humor,
as the mountain dedicated to hope is a crest so low
you barely have to strain climbing it on a bicycle.
A few heaving pedals before you reach the rise
will get you to the minimal peak of our hope.

But we reject most names given to us by outsiders,
mystifying visitors with nicknames so confusing
that they might never sort us out, which is of course,
the plan. We can Eee-ogg right in front of you, about
people you know, maybe about you, and you will never
know it, unless you are willing to peer in the mirror
and recognize your own most obvious compromising
traits, the ones you normally overlook with a quick glance.

When you see the six-foot guy named Shorty,
you'll think it's simply ironic, because you're
not from here. You won't know we remind Shorty
we know he's lying when he says he forgot his
wallet, that he's just a little too short to pick up
the tab this time, but maybe next time. He

agrees to be Shorty because he knows, as we
do, that the only "next time" is the next time
he touches his front jeans pocket, as if that
proves his report that it is empty again.

Even its transformation from dirt road to paved,
will not change the fact that Mount Hope is
forever Dog Street. The high density of free
range dogs defend their rough property and
prowl the street, chasing your ass if you're
unlucky enough to ride a bike through that patch
at the heart of the Rez, its deepest center.

There are no laws on the Rez, not really,
so the idea of a leash law is unfathomable.
A dog is meant to roam, and even if our home
is six thousand acres (a lot smaller than it sounds), it is enough
for our dogs to dream their doggy dreams of surviving.

They are members of their pack, thriving by their
strength in numbers, their willingness to chase
cars as if hundreds of their littermates have not
been left mortally wounded on our roadsides
by strangers who come out to joyride on our roads
in muscle cars where speed limits are only a suggestion.

For Dog Street Dogs to stop the chase is to give up
their identities, accept the collar and stand still as
their leashes are tied to rods, shrinking their territory
to a jagged circle of grass, dug up in desperation.

Early and Late

In the Red Album, two side-by-side photos of me
on our stoop, less than a year apart, reveal gaps
and stopgap measures we went through in the time
I was a baby, too young to understand struggle.

In one, Big Umma holds me on her lap, framed
by the rubber and spokes of her post-amputation
wheelchair. I have no memory of her whatsoever,
the only version of her voice I've heard is family
members imitating her super-draggy Rez accent,
as she fused sharp English words with the crunched
vowels of Tuscarora, to shape a secret code for members
of her generation as they felt their brains make
new patterns, trying to accommodate the world
they knew, crops and seasons, dirt roads and ruts,
and long stretches of woods in their shadowy density,
trees, bush, animals, paths, with the unfamiliar
world they were learning falling through the air,
in radio and eventually television transmissions.

I was a late arrival, coming almost five years
after the last expected baby, my brother
growing impassioned by lacrosse at the age of four.
My mother, carrying this unexpected baggage
in her forties, wonders how she's going
to afford his requisite Pee Wee lacrosse
equipment on top of the costly temporary junk
that comes with babies. So she works longer into
her pregnancy than most, leaving the other six
kids home with her parents to watch them,

as she cleans and cleans, even on her hands
and knees for the white ladies of Lewiston
who pass her dollar bills under the table, and
pretend not to see her walking the miles
back to the reservation at day's end.

They say they're doing the old Indian woman
a favor, really, some charity, letting her work
this far along, as they leave the house
to play Bridge (and prove they trust the woman
won't take their shit when they're not looking).

My sister replaces Big Umma in the second
photo. It is months later, and she is fifteen, same
place, same bundled baby, same attempt to smile
for the camera, but Big Umma has passed
in the months between. She even wears a sweater
in midday light, so it's probably fall, when bright sun
still can't boost the day above sixty degrees, and it will
be at least a month before we can begin heating the house
for the long winter ahead, so we each put on another layer.

She was fourteen, when I was born, her freshman
heart too busy, too full to add another unexpected
brother, another mouth demanding food we did
not have, another crying voice, demanding
a scarce sliver of attention.

She knew that I could sleep in a laundry basket
for a couple more months, tops, she knew babies
did not stay that size very long. Even diapers
progressed from Newborn to Toddler with stops

in between because among a baby's few skills
(consuming, eliminating, 2:00 a.m. screaming)
Growing is their number one specialty.

Like the Hulk, infants burst from meager offerings
relatives brought to the baby shower months earlier.
Those donations free them from obligation, silently
proclaim "we already bought you what we could
afford to spare," but later they do drop off bags of clothes
their own children grew past, waiting for the next family
member, sensing the desperation of new parents getting
ready to cut the feet off their baby's footie pajamas
to get a couple more months out of them.

I look at the photos side by side, knowing there
should have been one of my mother in the same
position, but I don't want to ask, because I don't
know which is worse: that we've lost the only photo
of her and me together in that time, or that one day she
discovered she was too late, with never enough leisure
time or energy to sit with her newborn in sunlight
and warmth in the months before I learn to sit,
and then stand, shaky, and take my first steps
on the reservation with my own two feet.

The Spoiled Bat

My earliest memories of my oldest brother are of those
photographs, removed from our real lives. He was
drafted into the army during the Vietnam War when
I was a baby. Our mother sent pictures of us to him
in Vietnam whenever she could, stuffing envelopes
with photos scarce as dollar bills in our house, ripping
open the ones he sent back, striped in red, white, and blue.

She hoped to show him how incomplete we were
without him, counting days till he came home,
waiting for his next installment, snapshots of him
and shirtless sweaty members of his platoon,
perched in choppers, grinning in the jungles
to hide their terror. His shining teeth confirmed
in return, that *he was* complete, still alive. Eventually,
he did come home and rejoined us, never mentioning
much about the war, instead taking new pictures
with us all, to show ourselves concrete maps
to our lives, all back together again.

By the time I'm in high school, we keep a loose box
containing this visual story of our time so far apart
we could not comprehend the distance. Pulling them
from the album and spreading them across the table,
a Tarot Deck, I ask my mother why I'm in more
pictures than anyone else. "You were the youngest,"
she says, "the one changing the most quickly. You went
from baby to walking and talking, developing your Batman
thing, all in the time he was gone. He laughed
that you always wore a cape. Guess he had no way
of knowing you'd be doing it nonstop for years after."

We come across a photo of me in a riding
Batmobile, cape included. It is June 1968,
and I am three. I can see the extravagance,
even now, that such a toy should have been
beyond our means. Everyone said it was proof
I was spoiled, having a Batmobile when we,
as a family, didn't even possess a car.

She says she took my brother shopping
the week he came home from Vietnam,
and when he saw the kid-car, he bought it right
then, using the Combat Pay he'd saved.
She told him to wait until Christmas, but
he didn't like to put things off anymore.
That picture was taken the day we got it,
and they say they could never get me out.

The next photo in the deck is my brother closest
to me, five years older, and our cousin, a year
older than him, with me in the middle. The three
of us sit on our front stoop, years before it falls apart.
We each wear one of the many hats my oldest brother has
carried home from the jungles across the world, these tags
of his time in conscripted servitude repurposed.

Between the older boys, I wear no shoes, one sock
tip dangles inches below my toes, maybe a soaker.
In this photo, though, others only notice that I wear
a mask. It's a simple number, black cloth, fixed
in place with elastic, the kind old-time movie
gangsters wear, to hide their identities mid-crime.
It doesn't fit well, and my head tilts up,
to find the camera through the eyeholes. I am three

here, too, and by this age, masks for me have become
part of who I am, so common no one bothers
to tell me I should take them off for pictures.

My brother continues to spend his Combat Pay,
expanding the map with each roll, a whole stack
of pictures, cousins, friends, kids from across
the Rez, showing off their own wide innocent
grins, these sweaty talismans perched on their
heads, hiding their eyes in the brim shadows.

All this time later, I wonder if I am the only
one understanding my brother is hiding his
face, too, behind the lens of a constantly
recording camera, progressing the story
of his survival, one frame at a time, before
cranking the film, mounting another flash,
and opening the shutter for an instant,
burning the thin film beneath, scarring
its surface, transforming life into proof.

I Believe I Find Evidence That I Am Not an Alien

In my endless study of the Red Album, every once
in a while, new photos surface. I come to realize
each Rez family treats photos like hostage exchanges.

You hear that someone on the upper mountain
has one of you and your aunt before she moved
to Vegas and never took root back home until after
her last breath. They will give it to you in trade for
one they've heard is in your collection, of a family
member in better times, different circumstances.

So whenever you open the Red Album
something old may be gone, a new
fragment of a past mirror found.

In my hands, I hold a moment: Again, I am
no more than three, in shorts, white socks, broken-
in black old man shoes. On my head sits
an adult-sized lacrosse helmet, my oldest
brother's, I think, and I hold a traditional
wooden stick, hands in proper cradling position.

It seems like proof I shared my family's passion, before
drawing tablets, pens and books, costumes, took
me farther and farther into a different place they didn't live.

My sister, glancing, says I stayed in the pads and helmet
only long enough to snap the shutter, another disguise
captured then discarded. In the next photo, I've abandoned
that disguise for one of my favorites, always reliably there.

I hold my arm cocked, an action punch frozen, as if the person
taking my picture is the Joker, the Riddler, or maybe the Bookworm.

I am wearing a standard Batman T-shirt, like millions
found across America in this period. Being the committed
sort, I am decked out in a scalloped Bat-wing cape.

On my face is a mask owing more to the Lone Ranger (that masked
man Indians cannot escape) than to Batman. My skull is framed
by a cowl, bat ears complementing my seven-year-old's grin.
My auntie sewed it for me, maybe from a Simplicity pattern. I am
ashamed when I see this photo. When she gave it to me, I criticized
the ears as too floppy, like a cow's, thinking she could easily modify.

I didn't understand they would stand up once I tied it on tight. I didn't
understand she had taken such care with this gift, to soften the blow that
she and my uncle would soon leave, moving to Vegas, never to return.

Official and Unofficial Covers

My sister in this photo looks up
at the camera, a textbook spread out
on the table, covered in an Official School
Book Cover. I wonder now where she got
it, since we were reduced to covering our high
school books in paper grocery bags, so we didn't ruin
them in the carelessness our teachers assure us
is our way of life. We have to preserve them, for those
who cover after us, even though they house facts
rapidly becoming lies of omission.

This photo was taken in January of 1968, so I know
it is one of those sent across the world and brought
home again. When my brother looks at it in Vietnam,
an automatic rifle his constant companion, will he know
the history book on our table claims there is no war, no
casualties in Vietnam? That there was no Battle
of Greasy Grass, only the Massacre at Little Bighorn?

My sister's hair is ratted up, like she's about
to step onstage, at the edge of the spotlight,
be one of the background singers, flanking
skinny white men boosting Rhythm and Blues
riffs from black musicians, in clothes two sizes
too small, as they strut across our TV, singing
about all the Satisfaction they can't get none of.

But she knows better, that her chances
of even seeking satisfaction are shaky
at best, so she sits and carefully protects

the school's books, in their plastic covers,
knowing we cannot afford to replace them
if she should damage them in some unexpected
but wholly inevitable typical Indian way.

She studies, and waits for the world to change,
with no knowledge of how she might be
a part of that change, beyond the background
singer life, echoing or harmonizing with the white
voices who have all the access to the microphones
and cameras, and transmitters, sending signals out
into the world, demanding the change we all know
would come at some point, maybe in our lifetimes
if we were lucky . . . or if we were not.

My Siblings Try to Find Evidence I Am Not an Alien

When my brother got a good job out of high school, despite
all the roadblocks that had been put in his way, he bought
the family a group Christmas present, a color TV. We carried
our old black-and-white model to my cousin's, across Dog Street.

It never occurred to us that it might be a challenge for eight
people (even eight Indians with their love of communal life)
to find shows everyone liked, and that our treaties with one
another would sometimes turn violent, depending on our passions.

Being the youngest, I had the least say, and
still hating all sports, I presented a storm cloud
of static in my fanatically sports-loving family.

My brother, purchaser, had implied final say, but he
was the generous sort. He noted that I'd taken a sudden
interest in hockey, hearing there was a team named
the Pittsburgh Penguins, convinced Batman's squawking
nemesis had branched into team sports ownership.

My siblings bought into his idea. They thought, because
I was tiny, that I'd be easy to reprogram, that my love
of graphics would lure me in long enough to get caught
up in the sport, to catch their enthusiasm like a virus,
lingering over my lifetime, as it had over theirs.

Because their humor cut sharply on the gullible, they
convinced me the Rhode Island Riddlers would be on
against the Penguins in a few games if I waited patiently.

It took me almost a year to realize no such Riddlers
existed, which my siblings found even funnier, asking
forever if I still rooted for my old team. As every sports fan
knows, the best defense is a good offense, or maybe
it's the best offense is a good defense. One of those.
          (You can see here that no matter how hard they tried,
          I was always going to have a different orientation,
          that my antenna was tuned in to a more obscure channel.)

After a while, I found ways for them to regret
their attempts to retune me (I mean beyond
my commitment to stay forever the alien,
forever the outsider). I started simply, tuning
to Lost in Space, or Batman, hiding the channel
changing dial, my vengeance drawn from my
underdeveloped sense of indignity.

But Indians are seasoned at double crosses,
always planning two or maybe twenty steps
ahead, and when my brother saw the gaping
hole where the dial was gone, he reached into his
pants pocket, revealed a pair of needle-nose pliers
I didn't even know we owned, and changed
the channel, settling into some game, taking
the pliers with him, at the end.

What They Leave Us, When They Leave Us

When you are born, a late-life "surprise," you are
surely the end of the generation, but still you raise
the occupancy of a three-bedroom house to eleven
people. By the age of three, your understanding
of the world is mostly limited to the one-acre
universe surrounding you and your family.
The back field of corn, tomatoes, and thorned
whips holding wild blackcap berries, is the world's
outer edge, and even these borders you see
from a high chair mounted next to the steel seat
of Umps's tractor. You two carve the contours
of his sorrow into deep dirt furrows, while he
tries to forget the loss of his wife.

For you, she is absence, personified, an indelible
silhouette of ignorance and lost opportunity,
but you carry her tribal identity, clan, history.
She has planted this seed for you to find, when you are
ready. Umps keeps a drawer of her jewelry that will never
be worn again and eyeglasses that will sharpen no one else's
vision. In the Red Album, tucked beneath his bed, she is
a series of fading images, unstable chemical color leaching
from them, the way it does from photos of a certain era.

By the time you leave on the school bus for the first
time, both grandparents will have left on their journey
back to the Skyworld, two brothers will have wound up
in Asia during the war, and a sister will contemplate city life.

People enter and leave the House on Dog Street
and sleeping arrangements change with each new exit

and entrance. Posters go up and come down, and you
absorb them all even when you don't understand
what they mean to others. What they leave behind,
when they close the door on Dog Street, abandon
the cradle of our singular civilization, might not
be theirs anymore, should they come back to reclaim it.

I gradually discover myself as family historian/
archaeologist, reveal Pink Floyd's *The Wall*,
Deliverance by James Dickey, a photo album
of endless dragsters and Buffalo Bills, the Monkees'
"Daydream Believer/Goin' Down." Because we
always claimed our own, I know who left
what behind for the rest of us to repurpose.

My oldest brother, spending his days in the open
door of a chopper across the world, sent home
a stereo, our first, along with requests that we pick
up each new Beatles album while he was away,
always planning for his return. Back home he'd discover,
all at once, the world for his ears had changed as dramatically
as his others. He left for induction before *Revolver* and six
months after he returned from his own not so *Magical Mystery
Tour* of duty, he got reacquainted with the Rez and his old
friends whose draft numbers had not come up. Untouched
by war, they remind him what it means to play lacrosse,
the Creator's Game, with a team he'd known for his lifetime.

When I was ten, he moved out, gradually, one load
of laundry, one album, at a time, until one
day all that remained were the sights and sounds
he didn't think he'd need in his new life with

his future wife. I inherited his half of one of the three
bedrooms, his centerfolds, a few scraps of Vietnam,
a back scratcher, an ashtray of a hand flipping the bird,
a used mortar shell. I went through our albums with
his signature and he had left us everything
from *Meet the Beatles* through *Rubber Soul,*
and then, at the end, *Let It Be.*

I asked him over dinner why he took all the Beatles
albums from *Revolver* to *Abbey Road* but left all
the early ones and the last album behind with us.
He said the ones up to the end of *Rubber Soul*
are too innocent, that the songs of them falling
apart were harmonies he knew better. Later he broke
our unspoken rule and entered my new room,
returning for the empty shell casing, planning
to take it to his new home. I held up *Let It Be,* but
he shook his head, said it was put together after
everything was over, that the real final statement,
the one he knew best, was the way they crossed
Abbey Road one last time, discovering once
they were there, it wasn't so easy to "Get Back."

Metropolitan Stadium, August 21, 1965

Either my siblings used to tell
me a lie, or I have willfully
misremembered the story of how
our mother took some of them with cousins
to Buffalo, where they sat outside Memorial
Auditorium into the dark night, traffic
screaming above on the Skyway, girls
screaming beyond security guards, blocking
the doors to my ticketless siblings, teenaged
Indians, boys looking tough in tight jackets, teenaged
Indian girls in ironed bangs and home-hemmed
clam-digger pants, and way too much drugstore bargain
bin eye makeup, as the Beatles sang to them, seeing them
standing there outside, wanting to hold their hands,
asking them for help, believing in yesterday.

But my family didn't yearn for any day
they'd already had, ever, relieved
they had made it through one more, before
they were old enough to leave our house, find
lives of their own. They listened to the magic
from the sidewalk, and I envied them and
the proximity they had to a history I wanted.

That is, until I discover as an adult
that the Beatles never even played Buffalo,
too minor a city to bother with, and I can
let it rest, until my friend Mick tells me one day
this story of his wife Mary and her family when she
was young. Mary's father did for her the exact thing

my siblings claimed (or I invented) but for her it really
happened. From the parking lot, even as George Harrison
plays a twelve-string Rickenbacker just given to him
by the owner of the B Sharp Music store in N.E. Minneapolis
that day, Mary and her brother don't hear Something New
Something New. Instead they drown in a tidal wave
of screams ten thousand Midwest girls deliver, wanting
release from their daily lives, the sedate world
of Minnesota. Mary (always more Monkees
than Beatles) is there because of her brother's
passion, mostly. Still, she knew she was a part
of Something New among the empty cars filling
Metropolitan's lot, if only in the sonic world echoing
in the shells of their ears, tripping the hammer, stirrup, anvil.

And in that way, I understand my siblings
needed to leave our life so bad, if even briefly,
that they invented a detour, taking imaginary
Beatles hostage, maybe after the Maple Leaf Gardens
show, rendering from air and synapse a world
where they weren't tied to a leaking house
and the unexpected infant brother they found
in me, saddled while our mother cleaned
the homes of white women who could afford
to ignore the traces of their own earthly lives.

Though I would have been only six
months old, according to their invention,
after all these years, I like to think
I would have understood their desires
and dreams, to convince themselves
and me that they had something beyond

the realities of our life inside
those crumbling walls,
and would have silenced myself
in the laundry basket we used for a crib,
allowed them this evening, conjured
from their impoverished imaginations,
which couldn't even take them the hour-
and-a-half distance to Toronto, giving them
something to remember, at the shores
of Lake Erie, a different barrier,
a better kind of screaming, release.

From Iron Man to Skywalker: I. Half This Blood, Half That

For one brief day, my father makes an appearance.
Everyone says he is an Iron Worker. Though I know
it can't be right, I sometimes imagine him in Tony Stark's
red and gold metal uniform, atomic heart and jet boots
glowing, distracting us from his expressionless cold metal
face, revealing nothing but the occasional bloodshot eye
and chapped, parched, bleeding lips. We are at my aunt
and uncle's house when my grandmother (his mother) turns
eighty. She only had three children, so he knew he'd be
missed. With the subtle approach of the seven-year-old I am, I try
to get his attention with the model of Mr. Spock I insisted on
bringing. He is the most well-known character on *Star Trek*,
pointy ears, checkmark eyebrows, and bowl-cut hair, dead
giveaways he's an alien. But maybe twice a season, he smiles
and laughs, and remembers that he is only half logical Vulcan,
and that the half he gets from his mother is wholly human. My father
beats the half-Vulcan with his lack of emotion for the few minutes
it takes for him to find my brother to ask how Pee Wee lacrosse is
going, then our older brothers to hear about their adult lacrosse team,
the Hawks, who play across the border once a week. Then he slips
a cigarette between his lips and says he's going out for a smoke.
With that one puff, he vanishes like Spock in the transporter
that has beamed him down in the few seconds I wasn't looking,
to another planet, where he has no history, no connection, no DNA
to scramble and rematerialize on a place where his prime directive
is to not interfere, to leave no trace he was ever there.

Hunger Test I.

At month's end, when the days outnumber
the combined goods in the house, and available cash,
which of the following did your mother serve,
trying to convince everyone at the table this
was dinner, for seven, six, five, four, three, you?

    a.) lettuce and mayonnaise sandwiches
    b.) government commodity cheese + elbow macaroni
    c.) ½ lb. "use today or freeze" ground beef
       2 tbsp. cornstarch + beef grease
       1 short loaf (day old) Sunbeam bread
    d.) Bisquick dumplings + chicken wing meat
    e.) all of the above
    f.) none of the above

Extra Credit: How many times have you
               made these meals now that you no
               longer need to compare the calendar
               with the cupboard and fridge, to remind
               yourself
                     of all
                         you have gained
                             all you have
                                 lost?

Show Your Work

Eel

1.

In kindergarten, I fail
to understand the prompt: "Draw
Your Clan." My clan name lives
in my brain, three-letter abstraction.
A helpful friend, trying, suggests
it's like his clan, minus legs. The rest
of the day I believe my clan is a species
of amputee Snipes, birds forced to sky
forever, forbidden from land,
symbols of endurance
or disfigurement.

2.

My mother explains we are not legless
birds, mutants. If she'd had a better education
she would have known the word
"ambiguous," not quite fish, more than snake,
but settling into her limitations, she says
we are among the few (the Marines?).
The last Tuscarora Eel died
a generation ago, so we are left
Onondaga Eels among the Tuscarora,
opinions dismissed by politics of representation,
voices silenced in air and water.

3.

An encyclopedia photograph
(not cast in Curtis's sepia) offers
jagged rows of razor teeth

set in a mouth perpetually grinning,
shimmering undulating sides, a long crest
of dorsal fin defining the spine, nothing
I've seen in any mirror. She explains
vaguely our clan belongs to a system
tracking families, and when I probe
further, she says we remember them
so we don't accidentally fall in love,
marry our relatives, ending by asserting
we have no more affinity with eels
than the rest of the reservation.

4.

"If I threw you in the dike," she adds,
"you would drown as fast as anyone
else," and I remember older cousins,
swimming beneath me, surprise
attacking between my legs, and suddenly
I rise, their hands grabbing my
knees as my balls collide
with the backs of their necks,
and they break waves,
toss me through air into deeper
water, probably watching to make sure
I surface, but only after some laughter
while I struggle toward light.

5.

In new, wet darkness,
I imagine my own Secret
Origin, taking water in, growing
heavy and cold, swapping air

in my lungs for another element,
discovering gills like Aquaman
or Namor, the Sub-Mariner, turning
inward, swallowing my tail, infinite
aquatic Ouroboros. Knowing
I had better odds of dying, facedown,
no voice to call for help, I am never
quite brave enough to try, not daring, even,
to open my eyes when my face has broken
the stillness of river water contained.

6.

Every now and then, I flip on my back,
close my eyes, ears below the surface,
listening to mysteries there, breathe shallowly,
stay at that level and float, wonder what it would be
to glide through darkness, knowing if I were
there, I would desire legs and lungs,
and then I fill my chest to capacity,
turn and dive, loving
and begrudging the ache I find
throbbing in my rib cage begging
for release, and I swim
back up, eyes still closed
wondering how long it will take
to find the surface again.

Tonto's Dog Street Cousins

Even before I have ever seen an episode, I know
who the Lone Ranger is. Everyone on the Rez knows
these three things by the time they can read and write:

1.) Despite the title, the Ranger was hardly
ever alone, traveling with his trusted
companion Tonto, all fringed buckskin
and broken English, a bare-faced Indian
who didn't need a mask like the Ranger to
seem outside the law, at the edge of civilization.

2.) Tonto, a.k.a. Jay Silverheels (real name: Harry
Smith, was Mohawk, born and raised on the Six
Nations Reserve, an hour from our home), first gained
notice as a lacrosse player, then adopted his nickname
(because his feet were so fast in the arena) as a stage name.

He first found work as an extra and a stunt man in Cowboy
Movies, slowly working his way up, being given line
after stilted line. His willingness to massacre the English
language regularly, eventually landed this role where, once
a week on the American Broadcasting Company, he screwed
up, needing to be rescued by his masked vigilante partner.

3.) We watched, anyway, however we could, periodically
manipulating the antenna the whole time to get better
reception over the airwaves, a clearer picture of his face, so
like our own faces. We knew his cousins living ten little Indian
houses down Dog Street from us. By the time I came
along, the show had been off the official airwaves for over
a decade, but I still caught regular syndicated glimpses.

Every weekday at 5:30, between *Batman* and the local news
reporting all the crimes and tragedy surrounding us daily,
we tuned in to his exploits. Sometimes, when I was brave
enough, I'd wander down and ask his Dog Street cousins how
he was doing, if they'd seen him lately, the way you'd ask
anyone on the Rez about their relatives who had left
for other places, different lives. They'd tell me he was
fine, that he'd been there at the table a few hours before me.

Only later, at home, when I told my family that
I'd just missed him, did they explain, laughing,
that he hadn't shown in maybe decades, that no
movie star would come back and hang out
on Dog Street after being away for so long,
after living that different life for too many
years to regularly find their way back home.

As I watch him now, occasionally riding into the sunset,
I wonder what would have happened if I'd studied harder
in school, if I'd believed then you could be an artist
and an Indian at the same time. How did he feel sleeping
beneath that Hollywood sign, making his stake with
vocabulary as limited as the cubes in a Boggle game?
How lonely was he there having no one to speak Mohawk with,
no one to count out the ceremonial moons each year with,
no one to light the path for him, no footsteps to follow
in except his own fleeting, gleaming silver heels?

Jaboozie Gives Me Two Lessons in Tradition

We are at that in-between place, no longer
kids, not quite teenagers. We've been playing
all day at her house halfway down Dog Street
from mine. She's been teaching me how to match
colors and tie knots to catch the hollow glass
globes used in beadwork. In the middle of her
rhythmic, perfectly gradient green beaded turtle
shell, she places one ridiculous bright yellow
bead, off-center in one plate. I point out this
error, trying to be helpful, because I'm not
beading, myself, worried I won't have the
coordination, patience, or endurance to complete
the job. She says in every piece of art you make
if you are Haudenosaunee, you include one flaw,
intentionally, so you acknowledge that only
the Creator can make something perfect. She says
the yellow bead is her signature mistake, because
yellow is a cheerful color, if nothing else,
the color of sunlight when the sun is shining.

Her sister comes in and sees that we've been using her
beads without permission, and in the shouting that ensues,
we get shagged outside for making too much noise. Sunlight
shines like a wall of beads, and leaves are brilliant orange
with that light blasting through. It's maybe Columbus Day,
and the world has not yet changed enough for us to imagine
Indigenous Peoples' Day will ever be a thing people develop.

I'm not an outdoor kid, and consider going home, where I can
at least stay inside if I want. But she offers to show me

something if I stay, if we can pass the next few hours together
while her sister cools down enough for her to go back inside.

We cross the bush line into the field next door, littered
with cornhusks, rotted ears, and broken stalks, because
harvesttime has come and gone. She hands me a couple
husks and says to carefully tear them along the natural
channels threading through the leaves, then teaches me
how to braid them into a fragile rope, and we make a few.

She grabs a couple more husks, this time studying
the shuck piles for some with a mysterious quality
I can't see, myself. Collecting them, she folds,
straightens, uses our new twine to tie parts off,
and several minutes later, she holds before me
a cornhusk doll, the kind you see for sale at every
Indian event all year long, an object of art out
of the scraps others have left behind. She makes
a second one, more slowly, so I can follow her,
learn by witnessing. This is one of the arts, one
of the skills that do not exist in our house.

Because she wants to know everything
about everyone, even those sleeping
in the graveyard on the upper mountain, Jaboozie
is already aware of Little Umma's reputation
for her cornhusk dolls. And Jaboozie also knew
then, that we lived in the house of Big Umma,
where tradition was considered a threat to our futures.

I worry about taking mine home, that my mom
might throw it out. Jaboozie smiles and says that's

the beauty. Once you know how to make a cornhusk
doll, all you need are these scraps people think
of as waste, to make yourself something new and
beautiful, a skill so rare, so hard to come by. When
I go home, I leave my creation with her. There are so
many obvious flaws, no one will mistake it for something
done by the Creator, but it is what I have to offer, a thank-
you for the lessons, the gifts I can carry with me forever.

From Iron Man to Skywalker: 2. Tanned Hide

At Indian Picnic, our rusted version of Marvel's
metallic hero resurfaces. My father is still an Iron
Worker, which is how everyone explains his constant
absence, that he exists in other cities, walking I-beams,
to build skyscrapers that would never let him in
the door once finished. Even in his wayward ways,
he knows everyone comes home at least for this
one weekend a year. I am nine, seeking relief
in the grove's thickest shade. My sister rests
from pushing her son's stroller and my niece
is restless, hot in the rawhide dress her grandmother
has tanned for her, burnishing it with the deer's brains,
and smoking it to cure, before adding beads and fringe
for her. He seems not to see me when he asks
my niece to give him a kiss. Even at four, she hesitates,
and because she has not learned lies we tell out
of politeness, she says he's too greasy. I tell myself
he can't see me because she is his first grandchild.
"Greasy" becomes our code word for the skin
shine we've all inherited from him, sometimes
looking like bologna left out in the sun too long. But in
that moment what she really senses is last night's acrid
beer, seeping across his face in the steamy July day
where we all look to reconnect, assert our shared history.

Wyatt Wingfoot Gives Us Some Four-Color Comic Hope

On page 18, issue 50 of the *Fantastic Four*,
you see him for the first time. The FF have just
encountered Galactus and the Silver Surfer
during their initial exploration of Earth, another New
World to conquer and maybe Devour, if
the Elements taste right and ripe for the picking.

A moment of firsts, when other worlds collide, Johnny
Storm sets foot on campus wanting to blend in like any
college freshman, as if others would not request that he
"Flame On," transforming his skin into a hot, blazing red
ember you would never want to touch, not for a hug, a kiss,
or even a friendly handshake to show you carried no weapon.

The Dean introduces Johnny to Wyatt, a member of the Keewazi
tribe and in Marvel Universe logic, the Dean suggests they room
together, to help each other cope, two freaks on a college campus:
a man transformed by cosmic rays into Flame Personified
and a Rez-Born American Indian, attempting college.

Though fast friends, Wyatt remains a fluke. His encounter
with the substance of a different world does not transform
him into something more than human. Because almost everyone
in the Marvel Universe is unfathomably wealthy, Wyatt belongs
to a tribe who discover oil on their land. Maybe his family's super
power is that his mother is not romanced by a white man and then
murdered a couple of years after they marry, once the oil shares
are considered her widower's property. Maybe his super power is
survival. If you are an Indian in popular culture, this is no small thing.

Hunger Test 2.

You have stayed the night at certain Rez houses, later
recognizing your mother said yes strictly for families
living the same ratio of resource to need. Because
you went to Catholic Charities camp with two brothers
from Dead Man's Road, you are allowed to go. Your mother
doesn't know this is a working farm, with a wood-burning
stove, and a freezer stocked with food from it. You've
been told not to eat too much, even if you want to, and even
if it is offered . . . really, especially if it is offered.

In the morning, you wake to a warm room,
filled with abundant breakfast sounds and smells,
the kind you see TV families eating, impossible mounds
of steaming food, covering a table that has been set
with cereal, mush, fruit, and next to a bacon-stacked plate,
there sits a carton of eggs like you've never seen, shells
the color of everyone's skin in May, Indians before summer
sun has baked us in its rays, but after the spring farmwork.

You want the eggs, but worry about the taste of brown eggs
and knowing that letting food go to waste is a luxury, what do
you do? Eat with risk, enjoy abundance, or claim to be full?

My Brother Quietly Tries to Wake Us Up

Mostly he listened to the Stones and the Dead, who
our mother observes are noisier than their names
would suggest. Meanwhile, the Rez falls in love
with *Billy Jack*, his beaded black hat popping up
wedged onto the heads of my brother's friends.
He has a clearer eye, saying the actor playing
"half-Indian" is all white. He says you can even tell
by the story, as it flickers across the Star Lite drive-in
screen. No real Indian, even the half variety, would
say that an Indian isn't afraid to die, like Billy Jack
claims in the commercials that run on late-night TV.

It's 1971, and anyone able to ignore the targets
that appear on our backs is a fool or has already
had some kind of brain damage. My brother
has a steady job and after summer school, got
his real diploma. He'd been thrown out
of school several times for "long hair violations"
until our mother tagged a white kid with longer
hair. She knew that if she made more work
for the office, they'd stop suspending him for
randomly enforced rules. He insisted he never liked
school anyway, but she said she was making sure
people wouldn't show him the door without a fight.

After that, he added Buffy Sainte-Marie to the record
collection we built, one black vinyl platter at a time, hid
the rust on his bumper with Red Power stickers, read *Akwesasne
Notes* as a subscriber, and bought us that color TV, hoping
we might see a real Indian on it, one day, someone not

just white, not just black, but like us, somewhere on
the lighter brown spectrum. We discover, late at night,
after all the stations transmit back-to-back National Anthems,
the United States and Canada, and then sign off, that stations
send us a signal, so we know where to find them. This Test
Pattern shows circles, wedges, numbers, and letters, and
for reasons unknown to us, an Indian Head, in full headdress.

As we stare at this static image, we realize that even on color TV,
Indians are frozen in the past, designed for a black-and-white world
instead of the brightly colored one where we live together, and breathe
current air, feeding trees and taking oxygen from them, an exchange
we did for centuries before others arrived, claiming new borders,
and driving us away because we didn't use land the way they did.

Proving Ground or Baptism of fire

You only figure it out later, maybe even after
you graduate. The Rez school is connected
to the larger district, like all the other elementary
schools in the region, but not exactly. It is treaty
funded, but only up to fifth, and from there,
you all migrate to the giant junior high and are
introduced to three hundred white kids, a handful of darker
kids sprinkled in, like pepper in the salt, and other
than the bus ride, you almost never see the twenty four Indians
you grew up with, from the western end of Dog Street
to the eastern plots of land, houses dotting Dead
Man's Road among the old-growth trees.

You notice in your high school years that teachers stay
put, but the Rez school might as well have installed
a revolving door for them. By fourth grade, you knew
who would not return in the fall. The younger teachers
linger for two years, five tops, before they find a way out,
transferred to one of the white feeder schools: maybe
making voodoo dolls of older teachers, taking their chances
with the sharp pins and bad karma to get into their "dream
job," in a nicer place once they are done "paying their dues."

Only two kinds of workers made careers at our elementary
school: the lunch ladies, the principal's secretary, the language
teacher, and custodian—those people from our community, who
found comfort and stability working with our nation's young.

The second kind were teachers who liked
to paddle us for minor infractions, ones who liked

to stomp on top of cafeteria tables and yell at us for being
wild Indians, and beginning in third grade, the ones who
monitored us after gym class in the showers, sticking
the rubber tip of a classroom pointer into our undershorts
on the floor with the rest of our clothes, separating some,
to show us afterward as a group, who had skid marks and who
had to return to the shower, to do a better job on their rear
ends this second time, using the soap provided because
"you're not *really* the bunch of animals people say you are."

Both lingering kinds believed they knew what was best for us
and the kind that left hoped we would stop haunting their dreams.

In this poem, maybe you are me, and I am you, or
you are you and I am me. I remember it differently
depending on what day it is, who I'm remembering with.

I Lose a Ribbon Shirt to Bloodlines

In a community this small, this tight,
if you are an outsider, you will be reminded.
We learn this early and are reminded often.
Some reminders are easier to receive than others.

We have lost the details of how or why two Onondaga
women arrive in Niagara County with the Tuscaroras,
landing on Dog Street at its beginnings. Maybe we can
be forgiven as we all came to settle here over two hundred
years ago. Yet because we are always defined by our mothers'
bloodlines, we will always be Onondagas among the Tuscaroras.

We learn this early and are reminded often.
Some reminders are easier to receive than others.

Every summer, when I was a boy, we received
a check from Onondaga Nation, lease payments
for salt mines carved into the Nation territories.
Dutifully, my mother would cash the check and
distribute it equally among us. Even at nine years
old, I understood that we'd be better off if she spent
the forty-five dollars collectively on food or heating oil, but
she gave us each our five-dollar bill, a concrete reminder that
we were each enrolled members of Onondaga Nation.

We learn this early and are reminded often.
Some reminders are tougher to receive than others.

In school, we learn Tuscarora language daily and culture
every now and then, when it makes sense to include it.

And though my father and three grandparents were
Tuscarora, and though the 65 percent of my body made up
by water is Dog Street well water all the way, like DNA,
I will always be enrolled Onondaga, the outsider inside.

Sometimes in Language class, we are told we'll be
learning traditional dancing: Round Dance, Smoke
Dance, Rabbit Dance, Standing Quiver Dance, Stick
Dance, Fish Dance, and the oddly displaced Alligator
Dance we borrowed from Nations in the south so long
ago, no one remembers why that happened either.
We are told we do not have a Rain Dance, so that when
we eventually hear a joke about one from a white person
(and of course, we will)
we will at least walk into it knowing this is our lives.

The note sent home to our families is a reminder
for us to bring our traditional clothes to school
on the chosen day. This is also a quiet criticism
of those families like mine, who do not even have
one ribbon shirt to pass down from one kid to the next
one waiting to grow into it for a little while and move on.

On dance lesson day, our visiting teacher, a professional
traditional dancer, is from the other side of Dog Street (the
"better side," I find out years later). She wheels in a steel
clothes rack where those kids with ribbon clothes (or those
with cousins to borrow from) had hung theirs that morning.
The teacher says she has some spares for those without,
but I can see the unclaimed clothes are mostly dresses.
Two boys shirts, both cut slim like me, remain, but
three of us stand, without. Beside me are two bulky

Baptist Church boys, whose parents would look at these
clothes, cluck absently, and dismiss them as pagan outfits.
One of them is my cousin but on my father's side, so
though we might sit together at lunch, he is always
inside and I am always outside, forever.

We learn this early and are reminded often.
Some reminders are harder to receive than others.

I discover, as she gives the shirts to the two boys who run
to the shower room to squeeze into them, that in this
Indian Poker game, a hand of Christian and Tuscarora
trumps Agnostic and Onondaga, hands down, every time.

I am the only one in street clothes, for our first tentative steps
in the Round Dance. This one every Indian nation has borrowed
from every other one, the origin lost in the universal. It is
the easiest Two-Step: one up, one over, one back, one over,
repeat, lock hands with each other, form a circle, let it grow.
It is supposed to bring us together, the only one I commit
to memory that day and I can still be confident now in this
move, stepping out, greeting family and friends, clasping hands,
moving one up, one over, one back, one over, again and again.

We learn this early and are reminded often.
Some reminders are easier to receive than others.
In a community this small, this tight,
if you are an outsider, you will be reminded.

Jaboozie Turns Me On to Deep Cuts

It's the Fourth of July, and we shouldn't really be celebrating, but even Indians can't deny the sweet forever taste of charbroiled hot dogs and ears of corn roasted till the kernels are crisp on the outside, exploding with flavor once you bite into them, surrounded by family in all its random variations, drawn home like magnets aligned to the same polar orientation, locked sturdy.

This year, I have found my way into the trunk of a giant Plymouth driven by Jaboozie's mother, stuffed in with her and her brothers, and my cousins and whoever else is willing to share space with the jack and the bald spare tire. We ride the dark back roads off the Rez to reach the upper escarpment, keeping the trunk tied almost closed with clothesline, so no cops see us riding where we are not supposed to. It's tricky since the car itself is already stuffed with adult Indians, which is, by this virtue alone, already begging to be pulled over and given an impromptu investigation, detained as long as the officer feels like asking questions.

We make it to the hill overlooking Artpark, the new place where they launch fireworks, competing with the city display that's been around forever. The blanket we'd hidden beneath inside the trunk is now beneath us as we watch the sky. Jaboozie's mom has the radio playing. Even though she's risking the battery, she feels we need the luxury every once in a while. It is the beginning of FM radio, and I am learning new songs I've never heard before, what the DJs call Deep Cuts. Though that label sounds painful, there is no denying the song transporting me to the Black Hills, home of the Dakotas, and men named Rocky, Doc, Dan, and a woman who must have been from a Rez out there, as she went by Magill, Lil, and Nancy, at the same time.

When it's over, I shush everyone on the blanket with me, but instead of the DJ identifying that song, something new comes on, a drawback of the current FM format. The assortment of cousins and friends crowded onto the blanket laugh at my panic, but Jaboozie tells me it was from the Beatles' White Album, and assures me we can play it when we get back to the house after the finale, when they let you know it's time for you to leave by blasting a hundred explosions at once, filling the night sky with smoke and echoes.

At the house, Jaboozie's mom drops us off while all the adults head out to do Rez laps, telling us not to wait up. Freddie, Jaboozie's older brother, doesn't seem to mind that he's just been drafted to keep an eye on all of us. As promised, we go up and turn on his record player. He has retrieved the album from his mother's collection. The cover is so blank it looks like a mistake. But Freddie has me run my fingers across the cover, as he puts the album on and lines it up, so I can feel The BEATLES in raised letters. This looks and sounds like no Beatles album I'd ever encountered. The photos included show them hairy and uncombed, like guys you might see walking up and down Dog Street looking for a ride uptown. Even the label is different from all of our albums, the rainbow border and drawing of the Capitol, replaced by the shiny green skin of an apple on one side, its crisp, pale interior, core and seeds exposed on the other.

Freddie says it was their first taste of freedom, that they'd chosen to make their own record label instead of being controlled by an outside force. He says he heard they chose an apple because it was like Eve in the Garden of Eden, gaining knowledge after her first bite. He starts the album with the first song on side one. Though the song I want to hear, "Rocky Raccoon," is a dozen songs later, on the other side, Jaboozie and her siblings insist there is only one way to listen to the White Album, from front to back. These kids from down the road have more music knowledge than I do and I intend to get an education tonight.

My world is changed forever, as if I have bitten the apple, myself, understanding this is a glimpse into the possibilities, and as we listen to the last side, they all grin, crowded around the speakers, watching my face when "Revolution 9" begins. It is not really a song, instead seeming like a nightmare made of sound, and though I am terrified of the mysterious voices saying strange things, moaning, screaming, the sounds of flames popping on burning wood, crowds chanting, horns blaring, when it is over, I want to hear it again. We sit around, listening to the entire thing from the beginning, making up ridiculous scenarios where we can't escape this song (?), agreeing we'd grow slowly unbalanced. We forget we are kids, alone in a house, not sure where our adults are, when they will come back, and not really caring. We understand the future is always like that flat, blank plain of this album cover, filled with mystery that we will never really see until it is right on top of us, confronting us with our own lack of experience.

Mr. Dressup

The Easter Break I am ten, my friends and I
hang around their house, watching terrible
daytime TV on the 13 channels we get. Most
of them figure that even bad TV shows are
better than sitting in class with a book open.

We are mesmerized by *The Uncle Bobby Show* and
especially *Mr. Dressup*, weird low-budget Canadian TV
shows. Mr. Dressup acts like no adult we've ever met,
pulling on costumes hidden away inside a trunk, pretending
this is the most normal thing in the world. He tries to pass
off the saddest plastic hand puppets as his "costars," Casey
and Finnegan. Uncle Bobby usually seems half-drunk so
you *really* never knew what might happen on any given day.

My friend Quinn suggests I stand close to the TV and we'll get better
reception. He is trying to make me more cautious about my desires.

The week before, I was my own version of Mr. Dressup,
playing Bugs Bunny in the school play, in a costume
my family made for me, going the extra mile, building
wire armatures in the ears of my costume, literal wire
rabbit ears that might improve a TV signal, like contraptions
they sell at Radio Shack. We had bought new material
at the fabric store that we had no business spending money
in. We sewed it all by hand, or rather family members took
turns sewing it while I watched because my skills with a needle
and thread were too sketchy to waste the minimal fabric.

With a new spare Bugs Bunny costume now laying around
the house, I had an idea my next year's Halloween
costume had just been in early development.

Every year, teachers requested volunteer actors
for events parents were invited to attend: Christmas
pageant; Easter program; Halloween parade. And every
year, without fail, I would vie for the lead role, though
I had no talent for memorizing lines or acting them out.
I tended to be the only one stepping forward, so I always
won by a landslide. I excelled in school and it did not occur
to me that no one else shared my enthusiasm. I'd come
home with a script and costume instructions, which my
mother ignored, driven by her own ambition.

She felt the instructions were insulting, minimal,
teachers trying to prove we could not afford
the commitment (more or less true), so she made
it a personal mission to outdo the assignment.
My kindergarten Christmas pageant role was
"shepherd" and the costume was supposed to
be a rectangular strip of white cloth, and a length
of twine to make the shepherd outfit we'd all seen
in a million Nativity Scenes up and down every road
off the Rez and in a few Dog Street front yards. She gave up
a bedsheet, and in our first family collaboration, made me
the full robe, equipping me with a shepherd's hook born
from a broken lacrosse stick with the catgut netting stripped.

At the school, I was informed I could not wear the robe. Everyone
else had followed instructions, so they were all dressed nicely, each
with headgear to show who they were supposed to be. Backstage,
I took off the robe and headed out with the others, only I welcomed
the Baby Jesus decked out in the Batman T-shirt I'd worn beneath the robe.

In fifth grade, I campaigned for the lead in *The Emperor's New
Clothes*, apparently the only guy in my class who had never heard

this story before. When I get home, my mother asks what the costume
is supposed to be. Reading the play, I understand what she's asking.
It is about a vain ruler, conned into walking naked before his subjects
because he does not want to reveal his ignorance about his tailor's claims.

The next week, my teacher assures me that like all the other years
I'd embraced with enthusiasm, there was of course a costume.
This time, however, my family had no room to show our ambition.
I would not be naked, of course, but underwear would be fine, a plain
pair of white briefs. I think this must be a joke, a test, to see if one
of us will go along with a school assignment, no matter how ridiculous.
My mother suggests long johns, believing I should honor commitments
I've made, but I insist I am not doing that, the same thing I tell my teacher
the next day. She tells the class she needs another volunteer because I
have chickened out. What she reveals in that moment, when no one else
stands forward, volunteering to be stripped of everything and exposed in
the name of education, is that maybe I wasn't quite the smartest one I'd
thought, for the previous six years, trying on costume after costume, hoping
to find the one that revealed my true self, too fearful when the opportunity arrived.

Metamorphoses

Now this is not about a man
who one day wakes to discover
himself a giant "monstrous vermin."
It is common in America to think
he's become a cockroach, or a dung
beetle, but for all we know, a mutant
rat could be what he discovers as his
own new body. It is unlikely, as the author
does choose to disclose that the new body
has a shell, wings, and other insectile
features, but if you're going to write
a story about a man becoming giant
vermin, how much further a stretch
is it to imagine a rat with a carapace
and bright iridescent wings? An armadillo
mutation? Would his family be less or more
repelled by the presence of such a creature
than a man-sized roach or a beetle collecting
animal droppings all day to build its kingdom?
We'll never know, since the original is in German.
What happens when you don't have an equal
word for translating from one language,
one culture to another? Is it always compromise,
always an approximation, a failure of imagination?

Already I've lost my way in this poem as
sometimes happens with metamorphoses,
mutations. When I'm ten, I go with my sister
and her family to her husband's reservation,
nine hours away, in another country,

where the Indian language is Ojibway,
and the language wiping it out is French
instead of English. We sleep in tents,
eat amazing French fries sold through
a Chip Shack window at the reservation's
edge, swim reservation lakes, and I unofficially
earn part of my keep, watching over my niece
and nephew mornings and evenings.

Deeper in one lake, Rez officials have
anchored a wooden float, with a laddered
diving platform. It's dominated by older
teens and people in their early twenties,
drinking and sunning themselves like lizards,
knowing the distance is too far for kids like me.

The adults have their own coolers and play
cards over endless beers, on ancient picnic
tables scarred with swearwords and vulgarity
since it is not considered appropriate among
Indians to proclaim your love, or even your
longing for someone, publicly, in speech
or the blade of a vaguely dull filleting knife.

I knew what it meant when I started
growing hair below my belt line three years
earlier, when I was seven, but I also knew it wasn't
exactly the kind of thing you casually announced
at the picnic table among family and surely not
among a bunch of strange Indians you'd met just
a couple days before, on this Rez nine hours away.
I alone know I'm too adult to hang around the little

kids, too scrawny and young to make it out to the float
without risking my own drowning in the attempt.

Though this change is my secret, I feel it's the sign
that I need to start acting mature in whatever ways
I can visibly show. I want to go home, but the secret
physical rush of new maturity aside, I am still too
young to understand that sometimes, someone takes
you on vacation to give your parents a break.
At my age, you can't know that when your mom sends
you out the door with a bag of clothes and one family-
sized can of Chef Boyardee Ravioli, to cover
a week of being away, she's asking your sister
to foot the bill to buy her a little freedom.

Six of us make this trip, layered in the pale '66 Mustang
with the dark blue door my brother-in-law salvaged from
some other pony that wasn't lucky enough to still be
around performing dark night Rez laps a decade later.

Halfway there, we stop to sleep in a store parking lot
and I awake to a massive thunderstorm sometime
after midnight. I've always heard you are safest
from lightning in a car because the tires insulate
you from a direct hit. Still, it's summer and I'm wearing
a T-shirt, shorts, and a brand-new pair of flip-flops
my mom has bought for this trip. When she handed
them over, I wondered what she sacrificed so I could
have them. Halfway between boy and man, feeling
both and neither, I try to err for responsibility and slip
them off my feet. They are rubber and I gently rest one
each behind the sleeping heads of my niece and nephew,
for whatever extra protection I can offer them in this state.

We eventually arrive at the unfamiliar plot of land my sister's
husband thinks of as his homeplace, though I don't know if
he ever lived there, in this little house his grandmother still
maintains. Though she has hip trouble sometimes, she
still insists on walking across the bridge between Canada
and the United States on the annual commemoration
ceremony, assuring the two governments that we
remember the details of our treaties, what was
lost and what was retained in our long history.

Here, I rarely go into the lake, avoiding strange creatures
gathering in grassy water. Mid-transformation, these
giant fist-sized tadpoles sprout front and back frog
legs, still propelling themselves underwater with
enormous tails, fleeing grabbing kid hands
eager to perform impromptu deep dissections.

Most of my time is spent alone with the radio,
one eye on the young kids' heads, making sure
they're above water in the shallow sandy edge,
guided by Top 40 streaming in from some
unknown tower maybe in Montreal or Quebec
City, "Wildfire," "Young Americans," "Listen
to What the Man Said," "Stand by Me," "Love
Will Keep Us Together," strung together so
they feel like a message that I'll get when
I can successfully tune in directly instead
of the phasing in and out reception you get
on every Rez I've ever spent time on.

Back at the little Rez house, I mostly try to stay
outside, and not add one more body to its overcrowded

state. The grandmother inside is not my grandmother,
but on the day she makes shredded moose meat in
mashed potatoes, she insists I join the other kids
in preparing my plate before adults come in and wipe
everything out. She is tiny, ancient, and still brains
and smokes her own hides, tanning them for moccasins
she makes to sell during the treaty celebration.

I wonder what she really thinks of all these
streamers from her own children, walking
through her door all at once, adding variations
to her family story every year, with each
new marriage, each new child. Surely this
isn't a vacation for her, as this house where
three people normally live fills with thirty
or more complications there for extended stays.

I imagine she accepts the inevitable, that she will lose
track of all these variations, and to her, this year, I am
maybe just one more grandchild she can't quite place
in the onslaught of young Indians in her family line,
reproducing, delivering new generations of feet to cross
that bridge on treaty day, confirming with the chain of DNA,
however it resequences itself in variation, that we are still
here, still standing, still walking, one resilient step at a time.

Lucky

Normally, for the two-week stretch of Easter
Break, I don't stray too far from home, staying
alone and watching lame daytime TV, while
my mother and a good quarter of the Rez head
out to a variety of farms in the region, to tie grapes
in the sharp early spring air. This means wearing
aprons filled with thick spools of jute twine, fingers
covered in aluminum rings with curved razor
blades, like Catwoman's claws. You stand
unbalanced in the rows of grapevines, toes
pointing skyward, Achilles tendons stretched
to endurance, and you wrestle with the dormant
grapevines, secure them to two rows of guide
wires, with the rough twine, jute slivers digging
into every finger, in places that will support them,
and when you are confident you've tied your best
knot, you rest your razor ring against the taut
twine close to the knot and cut it, moving down
the row steadily, vine after vine stretched out
before you like the one-point perspective
drawing they made you do in art class, to learn
how to use a ruler and not tear the flimsy newsprint.

Sometimes other Indians from down Dog Street
walk to our house, so they can all wait together.
My uncle chooses to work for someone he returns
to every year. It may be the same other farmer, but
since we never work together, I'm not positive.

The Easter I am eleven, my mother informs me, as we wait
at the road, watching icy overnight dew melt off the dead
grass of our massive front lawn, that this year I am Lucky.

92

Lucky that one of the farmers is Indian. His vineyards
are not on the Rez, but his house is, so he can be fuzzy
with the math, and decides eleven is old enough to work
for him, tying up grapes with all the other Indians looking
for work under the table, off the books, all mysterious
locations I eventually understand as "untraceable."

Lucky that he drives through the Rez at 8:00, looking
for Indians waiting at the ends of their driveways, bundled
up, with sack lunches in hand, so there is no concern
about a ride to work or a ride home at the end of the day.
You just climb into the open bed, and when it fills
with workers, he heads home and puts us to work.

Lucky he pays by the hour, and not the piece, she explains
pointing to the long stretches of sleeping vines. The white
farmers surrounding the reservation pay you a nickel
a vine, which adds up if you are a fast and efficient worker
but I've never done this before and am neither. I imagine
fights break out among workers, with some claiming
to have completed rows that in truth, someone else has.

Lucky he leaves the regular tractor shed door open,
so we have somewhere to sit for lunch, out of the wind.

Lucky he provides a Johnny on the Spot
for his workers, so we don't have to find
somewhere discreet among the rows and out
buildings to do our business when we need to.

Lucky his tractor shed contains benches we can sit
on and Lucky some of them face windows
where occasionally some sunlight will warm
your face for a few minutes as you eat.

Lucky the shed is cold enough that my sandwich
doesn't get warm and sweaty in the wax paper
for the three hours it waits for me to eat it.

Lucky I've already learned to like the bitter taste
of coffee, as the sips we share from our thermos
will give us some warmth through the afternoon.

Lucky he pays us through lunch. We get a dollar fifty
an hour, flat, for an eight-hour day. At five o'clock
he will park his tractor in front and retrieve his pickup
and five minutes later, we will have lined up his aprons
and rings, orderly on the lunch benches, now against
the back wall, so he knows we're not stealing them.
When he looks it all over, he counts out twelve dollars
slowly, methodically into each of our cramped hands.

Lucky this spring is warm enough to reduce frostbite
risk, and cold enough that the blackflies are still
sleeping maggots wherever they winter over.

Lucky I have two full weeks, which if I am dedicated
will return me to classes with an amazing $120 that is
all mine, to do with as I please, as long as I don't
buy something *stupid*, defined by her, not me.

Lucky eight years later, when I need something
called a Letter of Recommendation, to flirt
with the idea of a future beyond the orderly rows
of produce in need of maintenance and encouragement,
the farmer's wife is someone I can turn to.

Lucky she is someone who has stationery, whose
voice and letter and own life experience mean

something beyond our borders, and she can talk
about my industriousness to whoever might need
to consider these opinions of hers about me.

Lucky I am ignorant of this future, and just listen
to the crackly tiny AM Top 40 radio my mother
has brought along to make the eight-hour stretches
working the never-ending horizon seem to go by
a little faster, accompanied by stripped-down singer-
songwriters and glossy production harmonies that
dominate the radio, hit or miss as my taste changes.

Lucky the Beatles even five years after
they've called it quits, still play across the air
often enough to make me anticipate their arrival.

Lucky they continue to find new songs to sing
even without each other to help them along.

Lucky that I know they came from working
class backgrounds and that it is possible
that I will not be tying grapes for the rest
of my life, like the middle-aged Indians
rubbing liniment into their knees during
our half-hour lunch at noon, hoping
it will be enough to endure the day
until the sun goes down and the truck
backs up for us to climb into the bed
and make our way back home, huddling
together against the wind blasting by
us in the backwash created by the truck's
cab, where the driver sits alone, listening
to whatever radio station gets him through
the day, as he drops us off, one by one.

Lucky my last day of work is Friday and I don't
have to go back to school until Monday and by
then, the wild, earthy smell of grapevines waking
up is finally fading from the way it's ground itself
into my fingers and memory and I can be a school
kid again, paying closer attention to mastering
the lines of one- and two-point perspective
drawings to accurately map the world from
the landscape places I have seen and felt
it, stretching almost endlessly out
on the horizon, to an end point I can't
ever know as it keeps pace, its mysteries
always just out of reach, no matter my desires.

The Boy Who Fell to the Rez

Home sick from school, you flip through Daytime TV
not designed with you in mind: cooking shows, eccentric
Canadian kids' programs, and evangelist after evangelist,
trying to save your heathen ass, inviting you to send them
money you don't have in exchange for that soul-snatching
offer, and before they can reach through the screen, you find
Dinah! a chat-fest hosted by a faded blond singer with a mile
of straight teeth and a voice always on the verge of song. *Dinah!'s*
guests include the Fonz, almost anonymous without his gleaming
Brylcreem Superman hair curl but the last guest almost cracks the
screen with unexpected charisma and alien presence: David Bowie.

Your brother's been calling you Bowie after a recent Home
Haircut incident. *CHANGESONEBOWIE,* his only album
in your house, confirms the resemblance. Something lives in
his weird eyes the same way your eyes mutate whenever
you are photographed. You both cover tight lips for pictures
and you wonder if he also has a mouthful of monster teeth,
adult sized like yours, pushing through your boy jawline.
His hair crests like yours. You'd been hoping for a haircut
to make you look more normal, parted in the middle and
neatly combed down, but your renegade hair is like you,
and has issues with obeying any attempt at control.

On TV, Bowie's rubber marionette body moves with
his resonant voice that you hope might assert itself among
all those changes throwing your body into multiple
upheavals the last few years. *Dinah!* invites Bowie over
and he admires the Fonz, expresses his interest in karate, and
as you knew he would, pushes the boundaries of polite company.

He claims our public faces are just another mask, another disguise
we maintain so others don't really see us. The Fonz knows how to
play the role of charming guest, but the melodious voice
of *Dinah!* sharpens to razors, her "lovely host" mask slipping,
when Bowie says he's never been in love despite being married.
She wants him to affirm that of course every husband loves every
wife, for this is the script her main audience wants. Bowie casually
says loving with too much intensity is dangerous, because all masks
fall away when we love too much. More than his alien eyes and
boneless blinding white body, you understand his universal truth.

Your mother, working, only semi-sure she has a ride home
after scrubbing commodes spotless, fixes her *Dinah!* Daytime
TV smile, stretching a mile, because her employers want
to confirm she loves this opportunity every week.

Bowie insists the mask is everything, because to be caught
as an alien is to pay an even bigger price. You've known this
for years and you've already learned to be careful. Back when
third grade gym class introduced mandatory showers, you
quickly realized no one else had started the change you had,
and you angled every day, to face the shower wall, kept
a washcloth hanging below your navel when you passed in front
of the other boys in your class, and yanked your briefs back on,
quickly, even as they stuck to your still wet legs. Only then,
did you turn around to face the others and finish dressing, safe
in your kid disguise again. Your necessary costume remains
minimal, a small white cotton garment with an elastic waistband.
You know already that to be different is to be separated, set apart
from others, no matter how minor and insignificant the difference.

Bowie tells his host he's soon to star in a film called
The Man Who Fell to Earth, and you wonder if he knows

the secret story your mother won't tell you, not the dreary
clichéd one of God and Lucifer and Adam and Eve and
unquestioning sacrifice and punishment, but the traditional
one old Indians will tell you if you listen attentively enough,
about Skywoman who fell (or was pushed) from the sky and
survived her trip to Earth with help from animals, creating
the start of life in this place. This story your mother thinks
is nonsense, though she's willingly signed on for the Seven Day
Creation, the Fruit of Knowledge, the Banishment, the Great
Flood, the Destruction of Sodom and Gomorrah, the Red Sea
parting, its crushing resumption when Moses waves his rod,
the Transformation of Lot's Wife. You understand she believes
more in stories of bad decisions, ruin, and self-destruction
than those where people embrace invention and survival.

Bowie performs one last song, about our dying world, and he reveals
his eyes, his teeth, and the truth that we all need so many people.
The room housing your turntable is not insulated but you bundle
up, pull out CHANGESONEBOWIE, and listen to every song,
trying to keep that earlier one in your head. By the end, you've
accepted ch-ch-changes and understood the difference between
Rock and Roll and Genocide, and little by little, the seed of that
first song dissipated from your memory. It will take you
almost five years to discover it was called "Five Years."

That summer, you are drawn next door by orange bonfire highlights,
stories being told, stories being remembered. You quietly join, hoping
not to be too noticeable. Bowie slickly oozes "Golden Years," from
the glowing green radio straining against the bedroom window,
sending joy into the dark. Your cousins' friend has been teaching
you to braid his hair (because every Indian man should be prepared
for the day he decides to grow his own out and become more visible).

Everyone is quietly singing "Golden Years," and you feel confident in
saying how awesome Bowie is. The guy whose hair you're braiding
insists Bowie is not cool enough to sing this song, and you tell him he's
wrong and when he doubles down, you leave, mid-braid twist in the three
overlapping strips. He will have to tear it all out and start again on his own.
At the bonfire, you don't need a mirror to see your asymmetrical eyes,
your meteorite teeth, your hair exploding like a sunburst, to know you don't
need to bother with the mask. It does not fit around the contours of your alien
face, your foreign voice, your otherworldly thoughts, and you run through
the shadows, Bowie reminding you that you're untouchable in these Golden Years.

When *The Man Who Fell to Earth* opens, you discover it is Rated R,
and puberty-rich or not, you can't exactly show the theater ticket taker
how far along on the path to adulthood you are, even if you are only
technically eleven. You hear around that for a Sci-Fi movie, it is
boring boring boring but also unfathomably heartbreaking. The sleek,
alien Bowie has left his family behind when he falls to Earth. He has come
looking for water to save them. You know this story, for your drinking-water
well tastes of contamination most days. Bowie knows he's more
advanced, and should have greater advantages. Only after he is exposed
as an alien by the only person he trusts, does he discover that for all
his resources, and the ways he understands our world better than us,
he can never go home again. He has to live in this place that he's fallen,
keep his alien ways to himself, and imagine that one day, he'll be resourceful
enough to fall somewhere else that he's a closer fit for, if not exactly perfect.

This is the story you've been waiting your whole life for someone to tell you.

From Iron Man to Skywalker: 3. Public Assistance

The summer I am eleven, growing accustomed
to new glasses I've been told I'll wear the rest
of my life. Not this particular pair, I hope, as they
are clunky plastic frames. My brother says everyone
drafted into his unit in Vietnam called them "Birth Control
glasses." It's a joke I don't understand, but he says I will,
in time. Right now, I think of them as the Welfare glasses
they are, the only kind allowed by our Public Assistance
insurance and circumstance. We've borrowed a car
to hunt for my father. The options are not broad,
an anti-treasure map of the city's few Indian bars,
what my mother calls "beer joints" like it's still 1957.
These are not bars owned by Indians, of course, but
bars that do not actively ban Indians. Some even offer
check-cashing services, for a fee, and are packed
on Thursday nights, as it's the night most factories
and union jobs pay. I spot him, through smoky
plate glass fronting the Golden Pheasant,
like he is a display, encouraging other patrons
to join him in a round or two, or three or whatever
number arrived at last call. She leaves
the car running and sends me in, her canary,
asking for the twenty dollars we need to get
through the week. He pulls one, damp from
his pile on the bar, saying I had better not
buy books with it, that they're ruining my
eyes already, that I'm too young for glasses.

Wyatt Wingfoot Ends Up Singing That Same Old Song

After I discover Wyatt, in *Fantastic Four* 50, I excavate all
future issues I can find, hoping Wyatt reveals that he truly
does have secret super powers he's been hiding all this time.
At this point, it is suggested by more than one person that I should
give up the juvenile pleasures of superhero fantasies. Some Rez
men suggest other fantasies will replace them soon enough.

A few months later, Johnny Storm invites Wyatt as the FF
explore Wakanda for the first time, encountering
the challenge of T'Challa, the Black Panther, and
all the tremendous advantages Vibranium offers
them, secluded, intact in their secret kingdom.
Maybe a year after, Wyatt gets the cover treatment,
as he and the FF battle a giant Jack Kirby–style kachina,
wavy lines across its blocky, massive metallic body.

Inside, the FF head to Wyatt's Rez after an improbable claim
by his grandfather Silent Fox. That kachina, a Keewazi god, has
taken on physical form, causing death and destruction on their Rez.

And so the twentieth-century Indians I see in a superhero
comic for the first time have "gone back to the blanket,"
wear Hollywood headbands in their long hair, sit Indian
style, cross-legged, arms folded on their chests, refer
to themselves in the third person, have not discovered
the apostrophe, are called "born chieftains" and "warriors,"
are asked how they acquired modern weapons, endure
John Wayne cavalry jokes from the "heroes," and accept
that the gods they created will cause their doom.

Reed Richards, arguably one of the smartest men
of the Marvel Universe, insists to Silent Fox
that the giant kachina has been sent by a Keewazi
enemy, the Red Star, an invader government from Europe
(underdeveloped and vaguely communist to my kid eyes)
and that the Keewazi are safe from them. Reed,
Mister Fantastic, has found a gateway into microscopic
universes, but tells the Indians that Europeans greedy
for their resources can't possibly touch them,
and ultimately, because this is an issue of the *Fantastic
Four*, he saves them with his improbable super power,
stretching his body into unlikely shapes and lengths,
and then returning to his own identity afterward. He
doesn't know Indians do this every day of their lives.

And yes, I know this comic is from 1968, a time
in this country when some groups fought for civil
rights, to be considered the equal of whites, with
the same rights. But we didn't want to be considered
equal and included, didn't want to be considered
American. We just wanted to survive, practice our beliefs
as we saw fit. What I want to know is: wouldn't you believe
in a god who got tired of waiting for you to act, if you were
on the brink of genocide for 500 years, and because I know
this comic is from 1968, what I really want to know is:
when do I get to see the Indians as the superheroes, not
the super hapless, when are we the victors, not the victims?

How much longer do I have to wait?

Stupid Things I Buy the Summer I Am 13

Because I have never seen two hundred
dollars in bills before in my life, and certainly
never before in my own hand, I believe those low
denomination presidents are endless and self-
regenerating. Advanced math is already not
my strong suit, and it does not occur to me
that the paycheck of $224.00 every two weeks,
that seems to stretch out across a summer, will
only happen four times. I work in a garage
but will learn nothing useful about fixing cars,
pegged instead to do what all the adult workers
refuse, mostly cleaning up after their personal
habits and scrubbing school buses of boogers,
graffiti, and vomit, for thirty-five hours a week.

After two months, when it's over, I will have
collected just shy of $900, half of which will help
pay the bills, half of which can be used
(somewhat) at my discretion and unless
I want to be semi–bare ass in September, I might
want to factor school clothes into the equation.

But I am hypnotized by this gathering of these dead
presidents who wiped out most of my ancestors, and
it is now time to hold them hostage in the sweaty front
pocket of my garage sale Levi's, ramped up full
of puberty and all it entails and see how they like it.

Because I am not acquainted with the actual costs
of things, I have a series of eye-opening experiences

in a couple brief trips to the mall where my classmates
spend most of their weekends hanging out, which send
me back to the Rez with an entirely different education.

This poem could be a list of failures in understanding
how far apart my white friends live, when you're not
looking at physical miles. That list could include
the metal herringbone chain that loses its shine a couple
days against my skin, no longer looking like the gleaming
gold one my friend MJ sometimes forgets on the locker
room bench after gym showers, that he tells me was a courtesy
gift for being in someone's wedding, maybe a cousin.

I could cite the bargain leather jacket that softens
and melts back to its vinyl origins when I lean against
a heater for warmth, or the engineer boots that I discover
when a bus tire rim lands on them, didn't actually come
equipped with steel toes in the cheaper models.

And for when I'm not at work, the dressier suede
shoes, each slightly different sized that I learn to
swagger in, anyway, so no one notices how one is looser
than the other. Or the cassette player with one speaker,
because I told myself at half price, I couldn't hear the stereo
effect from two speakers that close together, anyway.

Harder to admit, the list could include the packs and packs of *Star
Wars* trading cards, building nearly three identical, slightly
incomplete sets before figuring out the Topps company
intentionally made some cards scarcer than others and a
singular card almost impossible to find (number 2, if you want
to know. Was that an inside joke on their part?). I finally get

one from a white kid in my class who was mildly friendly,
and who'd moved on to less dorky pursuits by October.

But I kept each of those purchases, willing them to retain
more lasting value than their makers had in mind. Planned
obsolescence and scarcity were for people with a different
life from the one I've lived from ages one to twelve.

The stupidest purchase I make the summer I am 13 is six
cheeseburgers, two large fries, and an XL Coke, hold
the ice, at McDonald's, because I want to know how
it feels to leave a restaurant, completely full and satisfied.

The next morning, hunger was back and my pocket was
slightly more empty in a way I wasn't ever getting back.

I Leave Formal Training Before This Opportunity Begins

We hear the warnings that too much TV will try
to teach young people, and though it is meant
to scare parents and grandparents about the power
of media, my family hears instead that this
is just good advice. They know how tough it will
be for us once we are forced to enter that world
and deal with all the ways we'll be modified
by all those other sights and sounds.

Life will change radically when we are forced
to abandon the Rez elementary school because
there are no resources to extend our experience
inside those walls beyond the fifth grade.

Like our older sisters and brothers, we'll be
thrown into the giant middle school, an onslaught
of other kids, mostly white, preparing us for
the adulthood we will inevitably face.

We lose Tuscarora language classes
just as they are getting more complex,
moving beyond the basic Word Lists
and example sentences we've been
learning daily since kindergarten.

I get reports from nieces and nephews
of all the things they're learning in Language
class now, while I struggle to make
friends in this new life beyond our borders,
and I want to Get Back, learn the whole new

sets of Word Lists and concepts they are
fortunate enough to breathe in and out every day.

Five years younger than me, my niece
becomes my teacher when I am babysitting
her and my nephew, every Saturday night.

Like me before her, she excels in Language,
telling me they are learning the Thanksgiving
Address. Because we've been so dominated by
the outside world, giving ourselves regular small
doses of it, like inoculations, I think she's referring
to Pilgrims and Squanto, the predictable
turkey, fixings, and pumpkin pie.

I don't know it at the time, but Umps has survived
a Boarding School too, like my other grandparents.
He chooses not to speak of it. Because he is a realist,
he allows his daughter's children those daily dose inoculations
of that world, transmitted through our TV, so we will
be a little more prepared than he was. He allows me
unrealistic dreams of Batman and the Monkees
for the thrill of being acquainted with the impossible.

On Sundays, we all watch a variety show
called *Ed Sullivan*. Umps does not grant
permission to see the Stones perform their hits
because some lessons are too dangerous
for young impressionable Indians to learn
from entertainment designed for white
people's freedom. He does let us watch
the Beatles sing "Hello, Goodbye," maybe

because he knows those two words will frame
each of our lives. Later, we see "Two of Us,"
their last video, promoting *Let It Be,*
quietly telling us for them it is all over, too.

We can always return, though. The records
are still there, but so much else around us
disappears unexpectedly. Ed Sullivan retires
and Umps heads to the cemetery on the Upper
Mountain the same month my niece, his first
great-grandchild, is born. He has no way of
knowing that she will grow up to raise
heirloom Indian corn, feed our people
and encourage them to join her in growing
our history and future in sustainable
sovereign gardens, braiding the corn,
raising it to the ceiling to dry and keep
us fed for the long winters until it is time
to head back out, and begin the cycle again.

A new local TV station comes live when I begin
kindergarten, another education. They call it
an independent but what this really means
is they do not have resources the major stations
do, so they rely on shows from the past, or other
countries, to fill out their days and nights. I learn
of Ultraman, Astro Boy, Prince Planet, superheroes
from Japan. They've been changed in some ways
for their existence on our TV, often looking
like white people and speaking a halting English
like the older ladies and men around the Rez, the ones
who dodged the boarding schools contamination.

I also get to watch the shows my siblings loved when
they were just a little bit younger, and we become
more alike, sharing a common vocabulary of *Lost
in Space*, *Land of the Giants*, *Voyage to the Bottom
of the Sea*, *Batman*, *Star Trek*, even lame game
shows like *To Tell the Truth* and *Beat the Clock*.

But we silently appreciate the terror of one show
the best. David Vincent, one sleepy night, on a dark
road that looks as shadowy as Dog Street in its wilder
stretches, sees an alien ship landing. He understands
immediately that the Invaders look almost like us,
but that they are really here to smile and gradually take
over our world and claim it as their own. No one listens
as he tells of the emerging threat, and the most he can
do is stay true to himself and try to get others
to take him seriously when he says they will
conquer our world and make us disappear.

As time goes on, even these shows disappear from
Channel 29, replaced by other programs that seem
familiar to others, *The Brady Bunch*, *The Partridge
Family*, *Nanny and the Professor*. *The Invaders* and
Land of the Giants become hazy memories we try to
retain. We become David Vincent and the Spindrift crew,
dodging aliens who want to collect us for confinement.

I eventually learn the Thanksgiving Address myself,
and it has nothing to do with the white national
holiday appearing every year in November. We
begin every day, thanking the people, and the animals,
the earth, the water, the air, working our way up
to the Skyworld, stressing and softening as we see fit.

I stumble, each time, and wonder if I would have
better recall, if I'd learned it every day in school,
like my niece just a few years younger, instead
of learning from the Beatles, how to say Hello,
Goodbye, and when people leave us, forever,
unexpectedly, to face failure and Let It Be.

Hampton's Shadow Crosses over Us Again

Traditionally, our communities were home
to strong roles for women, centuries before
America would discover itself and even more
centuries before it would discover feminism.
It was a given that Clan Mothers make some
of our most important cultural decisions, and
children maintain their identities connected
only to the inheritance from their mothers.

But among the infections Indians brought home
with them from the boarding schools was the belief
in "The Man of the House." Umps went away to Hampton,
a school to develop labor skills in freed slaves and
"civilize" Indians at the same time, even before there
was a Carlisle. He was part of the earliest experiment
in exploring advanced Indian education in America.

I discover this fact too late to ask anyone
alive how this history came to pass, but
it helps me to understand a story my mother
told me when I first started working in
the two months of middle school summers,
seven hours a day, and five days a week.

She said when she was in high school, she
and my aunt were sent to live summers
with white families on the shores of Lake
Ontario, so close but still too far to leave
of their own desires or choices. They stayed
until Labor Day, paid all at once for their summer

of servitude, dropped back off at the end
of our driveway, meager clothes and two
months' pay the only possessions they carried.

Umps, the kind and patient man who raised me
for the first five years, was a different person back
then, still harboring the influence of his Hampton
education. She says he stood in the doorway
as they progressed up the driveway, behind
the locked screen door, and would not let his
daughters in until they handed over their pay
for their live-in servant life for the white and wealthy
on Ontario's shores. She tells me this, using an older
campaign she's already tried on me, so I will feel
lucky I get to keep some of my summer pay and
lucky I will get to sleep in my own bed every night,
lucky that when I have time off, I can spend it
with friends instead of staring alone across the lake,
wondering about my next chore when work hours
resumed. She says he did this because times were
tough in the country for people like us, long before
the Stock Market crash and the Great Depression.

I wish I could tell her now that Umps was re-creating
the Boarding School "Outing Program" she would have
never heard of, in the silence of that generation. He
feared she and her sister would not be "civilized"
enough attending local schools, that Hampton still
thrived in his brain, thirty years later, with all its
hopes, all its fears, and everything in between.

From Iron Man to Skywalker: 4. Devourer of Worlds

At thirteen, guys I'm growing up with laugh at me still
carrying comic books around, telling me I should know
by now that no heroes are coming for us, that we are often
villains heroes rescue other people from. Still, I usually have
one, imagining what it would be like to finally have some say
in what was right, what needed to be stopped. When my aunt
and uncle magically return from Vegas for the second time, they prove
superheroes are a possibility. Their presence on the Rez somehow has
power enough to make my father surface from whatever dark
and secret lair he has that wipes his memory whenever he enters.
He arrives at the family reunion party, to spend time with his only
brother, knowing he'll be stuck with us too. I have, rolled in my pocket,
Fantastic Four KING SIZE SPECIAL 5, in which Mister Fantastic
and the Invisible Girl reveal they are going to have a baby. Their world
is full of super villains, like Doctor Doom, and Galactus, the Devourer
of Worlds, but The Thing and the Human Torch still celebrate the news
of this future arrival joyously. I wonder what that's like, since many Rez
babies I've seen announced have come unexpectedly, at inconvenient
times, followed by a worry about how the family will juggle meager
resources with one more mouth demanding a share. By then, I assume that
reaction was the response to my mother's growing belly in the nine months
before I was born. I notice my father's temples have started graying just
like Mister Fantastic, Reed Richards. I walk up to him, release the comic
book from its secure spot in my back pocket to show him. Before
I can even find the panel with Reed Richards's joyous face as he announces
their child on the way, my father tells me to put that away before anyone
sees it, since I am too old, by reservation standards, to be getting lost
in other fantasy worlds beyond our means, where heroes
with special powers conquer villains whose own powers seem
more immense. I never tell him he resembles Mister Fantastic,

and instead wander to the table where my aunt and uncle tell
everyone that they have to watch for rattlesnakes and tarantulas
walking outside, and that cactus plants are covered in millions
of thorns that work their way into your skin, even if you just brush
by them. They say it never snows in Vegas, and that summers blaze
so hot everyone needs air-conditioning units. I don't know what
those are, but they sound like devices that might exist
in the world of the Fantastic Four, something Reed Richards
would build, to keep his family safe from a dangerous
environment, so his children could grow, prosper, live up
to the joy their arrival invoked in all the adults around them.

Disguise

sure, at home, the old-time Indians,
those who still remember the harmony
my mother and her sisters made touring
reservation Christian churches in driving
distance, they still remember our house,
had maybe even been within
its confines before seasons and our own
diminishing will turned its walls from slats
to tar paper to plasterboard to imagination and paint chips,
those old-time Indians could keep a secret among
themselves knowing their own cardboard homes, and among
themselves, still call me Batman remembering
dirty towels, tattered cast-off chiffon kerchiefs,
occasional Goodwill Halloween costume accessory
and any other piece of fabric
I tied around my neck for more years
than the indulgence of children could sustain.

Maybe they knew how pathetic
it was to maintain an identity
whose alter ego was that
of a millionaire, for our house
was sure Stately Wayne Manor
in the most impervious of disguises.

If this house had a Batpole,
it would have led to the deep
well filled with cold
kerosene-laced water
and as I slid down,

past rotting floorboards
and bones of rats and cats
mingling amid worms and beetles
my lungs would fill
chill blood and bronchi
until I lost consciousness
and dreamed of other places
where people did not understand
the desire to reinvent oneself,
imagine a different bloodline,
have compassion for the secret
identity and the signal
in the sky I scanned
for every night.

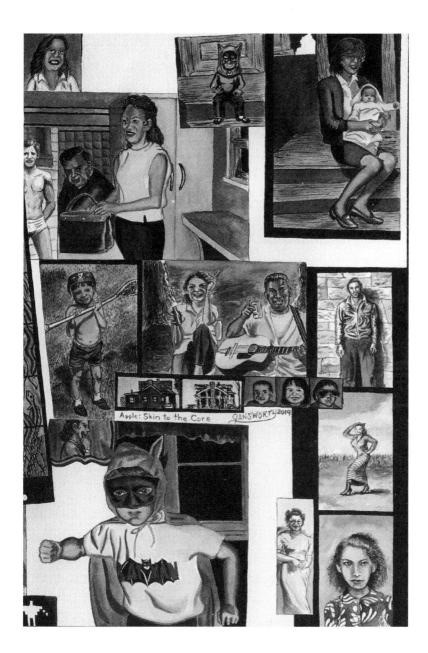

Apple: Skin to the Core   JANSWORTHY 2019

Masks Unmasked

1.

Before I was born, Haudenosaunee communities grew tired of anthropologists and ethnographers. They told us they were helping us preserve our cultures, but we said we were just fine. Two opposite statements. Could they both be true? Could they both be untrue? When did this gap grow so large? Maybe when city Indians discovered False Faces, ceremonial masks, displayed in museums. They protested, explaining that the masks housed living spirits and needed to be treated as such. They were told the masks were acquired through legitimate channels and also, they enriched American culture, like that was an answer. Maybe the gap expanded when we discovered ceremonial songs in a breakfast cereal commercial.

Our leaders have now made formal statements, condemning the use and information about the masks, beyond the private societies they belong with. People from Haudenosaunee communities, arriving at college, have ripped images of False Faces from library books, releasing the spirits within. The spirits are so entwined with the masks, that they inhabit the wood from the first shaping strike, inhabiting even photos. A publisher has let a book on them go out of print rather than continue to deal with this.

2.

This secrecy is not universal among the people of my communities. Some take their chances. Carvers who gave or sold their masks to ethnographers knew they would enter a museum's collection. They knew the power of the mask, but they made choices about putting food on their tables. A Dog Street man had a four-foot-tall mask mounted next to his front door the entire time he lived there. On some Saturday mornings, between superhero cartoons, Canadian TV broadcast an educational film, showing a Mohawk man carving a mask into a living tree and eventually cutting the finished mask away, releasing it. At nineteen, I entered the Indigenous Shop at Eaton's in Toronto, to see a selection of False Faces lining one wall, bar-coded for sale.

But by now, Eaton's has gone bankrupt and disappeared from the planet, and the little Dog Street house decorated with the gigantic mask has fallen into the ravine it was perched on.

3.

So much of my culture feels on the verge of vanishing. I wonder what part of that I'm contributing to with my own lack of knowledge. I've seen faces in the world around me my entire life, in trees and bushes, mountainsides, and crushed stone in my old driveway, in gaudy curtain designs, in swirls of carpeting, in clumps of ashes, in wood grain on a tiger maple guitar, in the waves of the river. Maybe this is true for everyone, but when I point out faces, showing the eyes, nose, and mouth I see in a pile of leaves, or in rumpled clothes, friends shrug shoulders.

Like every kid, I've been drawing since I was two. At some point, most move on to other things, but a few keep drawing, eventually painting, maybe sculpting. Faces have been my subject. They say that mask makers are chosen by the Spirit World, and that masks come to them in dreams or visions. The dreamers then join a medicine society. My visions arrive in broad daylight, not dreams, but maybe I'm supposed to ignore these inspirations. Because our leaders have made clear statements, I never draw False Faces, not even for myself, not even for practice. To draw them is to bring them to life, and because the place I grew up does not carry on those traditions, I'm not likely to ever be a member of a medicine society. A pen, a brush, can be dangerous weapons, or shields for survival. I use them with care.

What happens when you've been chosen to receive a message, but there's no one to help you translate it? No way to pass it on? Somehow, I've become a medicine society of one. How do you heal when you don't know the sickness?

The world of our dreams and the physical plane are separated by the thinnest of veneers. Dog Street and America are separated by an invisible, nearly insurmountable wall, and I have the smallest length of rope to try to make that climb.

That's all I can say, and I'm not even sure I haven't said too much already. If I have, I apologize to anyone who feels they've been violated. But this is my story, not yours, my message to receive and interpret. Maybe in part because of this secrecy, certain other things were inevitable.

4.

My cousin Thor (not his real name, of course), almost a decade older than me, a dedicated visual artist, used his bedroom walls as his primary art surface. I studied his beautiful charcoal drawings of eagle dancers, thunderbirds, flying eagles, and False Faces. He chose to live a little more dangerously than I did. He was also a lot older, with adult hand-eye coordination.

Inspired, I drew on my bedroom wall, in permanent Magic Marker. You would think the word "permanent" should have helped me think things through. Until our house burned down, from the top of the stairs, a cock-eyed Darth Vader presided over my mom's Friday and Saturday night poker games. Vader's gleaming metal skull, even poorly rendered, spooked my aunt, so she always sat where she couldn't see it, convinced *Star Wars*, like *The Exorcist* and *'Salem's Lot*, and *Carrie*, and anything else I loved, was the work of the devil, and that I was playing with fire. She tended to see the devil everywhere, but especially lurking inside me and my ideas of fun.

5.

Like KISS, for example. Sure, KISS was big in a lot of places, but nowhere as huge as they were on the reservation, even long after they'd disappeared from most pop culture landscapes. When I was twelve, my uncle took two of his boys and me to the ALIVE II tour in Buffalo, despite my aunt's protests about the road to Hell. We didn't understand General Admission tickets, so when we got there less than an hour before showtime, we wound up in the highest seats, furthest from the stage, where all the pot smoke had risen before the opening act wrapped up their set. So my clothes smelled like a concert, my ears buzzed with the loudness, but we didn't see a ton beyond the giant blinking-light letters, the occasional burst of flame, and tiny gleaming figures across the arena. But fans had mastered makeup. The arena was filled with thousands of KISSes, a new tribe, with its own set of rituals we were just learning.

I babysat my sister's kids every Saturday night and drafted them into living room mime performances as KISS. Every Saturday night my niece, nephew, and I rocked and rolled all night, with pots for drums, and lacrosse sticks for guitars. In my record case, I brought colored lightbulbs, a set of garage sale tempera paints, and an eyebrow pencil I'd lifted from my mom.

My niece and nephew claim I invented a finale. We didn't use the household chemical flame-thrower my brother taught me how to make, but we reinvented ourselves, drinking "poisoned Kool-Aid" and collapsing on the floor before their bedtime. I have no memory of this, no idea where I would have gotten such an idea, but I have no doubt that it's true. On Saturday nights, we wore worldwide rock star masks and then, I washed the paint from our faces and put my niece and nephew to bed. Sometimes I crept to the small bedroom they shared and watched them sleep, wondering what their lives were like. Their trailer was small, and when the furnace fan clicked off, the temperature dropped quickly. But they lived so much closer to twentieth-century America than I did.

One Saturday, my sister showed me a smudged towel, asking me what it was. I knew it was black tempera, as did her kids, but I claimed it was mud, and as soon as they left for bowling, we vowed to one another that we'd be more cautious. I experimented with different substances during the week, whatever might be easier to clean. The black was tricky, but the white was almost impossible. Pepsodent toothpaste gave a perfect, almost glowing surface, but its cleaning agent burned your eyes in less than a minute. You could be white, but it hurt like hell, and you had to wash it off immediately and be your plain old Indian self.

6.

I grew used to going back and forth, being two different people. My sister and her family had a flush toilet and a bathtub and a shower, and they could use these whenever they wanted. Even as a babysitter, I looked forward to my Saturday nights living in the twentieth century. My brother-in-law used to pick me up a half hour early, so that I could shower while their kids ate supper and they finished getting ready.

Leaving my sister's trailer when they'd return home, I usually stopped to use the bathroom one last time and run my hands under the warm water. In a few minutes, I'd go back to my house with the giant holes in the roof, the outhouse, and the hand pump out back. On Sunday nights, I'd pump water, heat it on the stove, and bathe in stages, with pans, so I'd be ready the next day in my schoolkid costume, mask firmly in place, the one that made it seem like my house was just like everyone else's, waiting for the next Saturday night.

In Spencer's, I Become Someone Else for Under Ten Dollars

I hear around school it's the place
where everyone gets their Fake ID and
I've been going there since the first days
of the mall. Right next to Recordland
it's always dark to show off all
the trendy lights you can't afford, lava
lamps, fiber-optic explosions of shifting
colors, strobes, colored glass bulbs with dancing
filaments. I always hurry past the mid section
wanting not to be observed among the shelves
full of adult gag gifts, hinting at the mysteries
of people's lives joined behind closed doors.
The back is filled with carousels of posters,
giant decks of cards featuring every sweating
rock star you know. The Who, the Guess Who,
the Stones, Queen, Rush, and each individual
member of KISS hidden behind their signature
disguises: the Demon, the Catman, the Spaceman, the Star
Child. Everyone knows rock stars always change
their identities. David Jones, to avoid being
mistaken for a Monkee, rebrands himself,
inspired by the deadly blade of the Bowie knife.

I scour the store, looking for the place
where they offer the Fake IDs, guessing
wrongly it will be a booth manned by a shady
character you wouldn't want to run into
in virtually any other circumstances.

Eventually, I find the slim plastic bag, stapled
with a cardboard header, holding a printed
card and two sheets of transparent plastic,
each with one side sticky with glue.

The instructions are simple:
GLUE YOUR PHOTO HERE
TYPE YOUR NAME
TYPE YOUR ADDRESS
TYPE YOUR BIRTH DATE
CENTER THE CARD ON ONE
ADHESIVE SHEET
CAREFULLY SEAL THE CARD
WITH THE OTHER ADHESIVE SHEET
TRIM TO FIT

The only lie I need is a birth date
from a few years earlier, but I know
just one person with access
to a typewriter, a Rez girl
from one road over, walking
distance from Dog Street
who worked in the high school office.

She knows why I want to age myself
up a little, and when she passes the card
back to me, I am someone else, older,
yes, but I also have a different name,
an address from some other place, added
by her inspiration and invention.

She tells me if I'm planning to sneak
off the Rez and into bars, I will be better
off the less Indian I seem.

Before I can protest, she shows me
her own. She's made us brother and
sister, sharing a nonexistent address
beyond the borders of the Rez, a shared
life where our familiar histories disappear.

From Iron Man to Skywalker: 5. Amputation Scars

I am fifteen, shooting pool at my uncle's before the sun
goes down, since he has no electricity. He sits outside
in his chair beneath a tree that offers only the saddest
of shade, and shouts to someone rounding the corner
of his house. I am secretly hoping the new guest
has a six- or twelve-pack with him, not because I want
one, but because after my uncle has downed a few, he is
more likely to pick up the guitar he plays less
and less, the older I get. I can't see the person,
through the screen door, and don't want to appear
nosy, until my uncle starts talking me up, as an artist,
like I am some new product, a better deodorant,
a toothpaste to make your teeth whiter, a liquid
wax that will take away the yellow on your floor.

He has done this most of my life, fairly often
lying about my abilities. Sometimes I help him
shop for monthly groceries, since his balance
with a wooden leg is not what it should be. I have
helped him undress and put his leg within reach
some nights when he's too unsteady to do it
himself, and I know the puckered, round scar, like
the end of a sausage. Though he mostly does not
discuss the limits of his amputation, I see how he rubs
it with sharp liniment to ease the ache on rainy dark
days, in his house with no electricity, no insulation
beyond the minimum of the two rooms he spends most
of his time in. He tells a cashier I can add the amounts
of his purchases faster and better than her cash register,
though I fail to meet the skills of her scanner,

and I can read without the benefit of a machine
the annoyance on her face, no price check
needed there. I know what is coming, and I set
the pool cue down when he yells my name
and tells me to go home and get my folder
of drawings to show all I have done and can do.

My father sits in the other chair, looking more
eagerly at the sweaty can of beer in his hand than
at me when I pass through the screen door. He says
he's curious. I know my grandmother has done some
painting, a skill she learned at Carlisle, because we still have
one of the paintings she did of him, when he was a young
man, posing in a lacrosse uniform, irritation leaking across
his face at being forced to stand still for so long, posing.

I understand it's possible they want a few minutes to talk
shit about my mother because she and her brother have
gotten along almost as roughly as she gets along with
my father. I run down the path and into our home
where she is washing dishes. She asks where I'm going
with the big sturdy folder she's found for me to hold
my drawings, and I tell the half-truth that my uncle has
asked to see them. Through the steam of boiling water
she pours on our dishes, sanitizing them, she grunts,
knowing somehow that my father is there.

She stays silent knowing I will receive when I get
there, indifference, criticism, and finally a suggestion
that I quit drawing "jack-off pictures," and maybe capture
Indians instead. I see the drawings through his eyes. These
are not images of glistening heroes, suave vampires,

glamorous celebrities, but documents of ideal bodies
in impossibly tight, revealing clothes, not the battered
and bruised ones our lives usually give us. Though I have
never seen my father's feet, ever, or even seen him without
work boots on, I know he hobbles a little, because an I-beam
he was carelessly hoisting, in his cocky way, fell on his
steel-toed work boots, cutting off his pinkie toe. They had
to pour blood from his boot when they got him to a hospital.
His body is as incomplete as our family photos, but my mother
says he has no way of understanding that, never big on metaphor.

The treatment my uncle uses on his stump is a short cylindrical bottle
with a round sponge applicator tip capping it. You tip it upside down,
rub it on scars, and aches, allowing it to seep through the applicator.
He says the liquid heats up on contact with air and confuses your scar
tissue with warmth, allowing it to forget for a while how it feels. It
has the unlikely name of Absorbine Jr. (though no one ever mentions
Absorbine Sr. What aches does it relieve? What scars does it confuse?).

The next time I help my uncle with groceries, maybe I could shoplift
a thousand bottles, one for each person on the Rez, or maybe
just one bottle, slid neatly into the front pocket of my Levi's.
With that meager offering, I could rub two patches of a U.S. map,
one where we live, and one on Carlisle, Pennsylvania, to see if their
scars would be confused enough to allow them to forget the origins
and nature of their enflamed topography for a while.

Reception

I am sixteen and am employed
at a garage in a job requiring nothing
but a good back and a family
living below the poverty line.

It's summer and I arrive
at work every morning at six
which keeps me home
most nights instead of running
with my cousins or whoever
else might have money
for a twelve-pack and enough
gas to make it
to the store just off
the reservation specializing
in cheap, ice-cold beer
proving there is truth
in advertising on occasion

and on those nights I pay
my mother's entry to BINGO
where she snaps chips
and bleeds minimal dreams onto squares
filled with random combinations
of hope and desperation and lies—
we know that spot in the center
is never free, while I smoke
cigarette after cigarette and watch
our ancient television phase the summer
reruns in and out of the previous
year I was too tired to stay awake for.

"What did we win tonight," I ask,
when she is dropped off at the end
of our driveway. I've already removed
every cigarette butt that had been
mine, sifted out the right percentage
of ashes, so we can continue
to pretend that I don't smoke and
continue to pretend we're going to hit
it big one day and change our station.

"Same jackpot as always," she says,
lighting her own cigarette, so it will
seem like the haze is hers alone. This is
our nightly contract, our constant
solace for the wishes we don't even
dare to articulate to each other for fear
they will go up in the same smoke we
pump into this room every day.

She never fills all the holes, brings home
that astronomical two hundred and fifty
but we finish each night satisfied,
dreams undelivered but intact
in the ephemera waiting
for those numbers to align
somewhere in the range of our rusting
and broken antenna waiting
for the interference to pass.

Jeannie Teaches Me Some Moves I Don't Know

Theirs is not a rock
and roll house. They want
nothing to do with guitar
and drum solos, flash pots,
rear-screen projections,
blood-spitting, fire-breathing,
and other stage antics
I gravitate to.

She is two years younger
than me. I am friends with her
brother, mostly, and I have visited
this family for many of my sixteen years.

Here, rhythm is everything,
and their mother sits
on the couch, casually
threading the catgut web
of a lacrosse stick's cradle,
and her dad recites, cackling
wildly, from his *1001 Dirty Jokes*
Book, asking all of us if we got
that last one, and as we have all
sprouted beds of hair below the belt line
by then, of course we got it
and just choose not to discuss
the sudden erections, intruding
on our lives, the methods we have
taught ourselves to deal with them.

A couple more years down
the road, their cousins, friends,

and yes, they as well, will laugh
when I have gained confidence
to dance on my own, busted in
borrowing moves from the Solid Gold
Dancers for "Eye of the Tiger."

Her brother Quinn will laugh
the hardest because he always
wants you to know who controls
all of our situations together,

but that first night, everyone on
the floor except me, Jeannie came,
sat down, said it's easy, pulled
me up, and commanded I listen, listen to that
beat, move one foot in time, you can
do that, then the other.

And suddenly, together, we lived in "Funkytown"
her small kindness seeded, on their sloped living
room floor, allowing me the possibilities
of the opened hand, the company of bodies,
minds, in synchrony, rhythm, harmony.

How Jaboozie and I Almost Lose It

We have known each other most of
our lives, because our families are
entwined in ways too complex for
anyone outside the Rez to fully
understand, let's just say neither
of us can remember but know
it was always inevitable.

We are two years apart, which can
seem like a canyon in elementary
school, but when two people live
in such a tiny community who
both love books and who both
have a knack of asking questions
that piss others off, they would be
bound to find each other, even if
family ties hadn't made it inevitable.

Over years, we sometimes get left behind
or are told to stay because we're not wild
enough, though we have both refused to
back down to liars who thought they
could intimidate us into silence.

Every year, the swamp deep in the Rez burns,
and we never know if someone has set it or
it's an act of God. Because we both live in
century-old houses, we have a vested interest
in this story when it flares up late every August
just before school starts and lingers stronger

and weaker, deep into September, an asthmatic
dragon hiding out in the wild Rez's southern woods.

Guys go by the truckload, hanging out open beds,
and open windows, but we have never seen it up close
and in person, only the long wall of rising smoke announcing
that year's major fire before the sirens blow for the volunteers.

The year she graduates, we decide to chase the smoke
for once and see the flames for ourselves, firsthand.
We start on the paths we have used all
our lives to get to and from each other's
houses and then step deeper into the canopy
of trees and brush, crash through the green
ocean of a thousand umbrella plants blooming
in the gloom as if there was no such thing as the sun.

Coming upon the fire, we feel let down, somehow
expecting swamp flames to look different, because
of the way everyone says it's too dangerous to be in.
We walk right in, feel the heat through our jeans
and sneakers, hear individual pops and cracks as dry
wood flashes and burns to the core, instead of the dull
distant roar that usually accompanies the southern
glow, like an Aurora that has lost its way.

We ignite the ends of dead branches
and write fleeting bright orange ember
messages in the blue sky, heat burning
and fading on our retinas like a flashbulb.

Growing bored, we discover the danger
no one has shared details of, assuming

we'd never be stupid or brave enough
to ignore their warnings or take their word.

The fire has surrounded us like we are singers
for a giant blast-furnace Round Dance of flame
and smoke. The sky above us darkens like an eclipse,
and the air lung-punches us for cockiness. She says
that, as always, I should have listened to her before.

Two years earlier, she tried talking me into joining track
with her, the easiest sport to letter in. She knew the rest
of our schoolmates branded kids from the Rez as lesser,
sensing it even when people denied their opinions to our
faces. "Track" was one of her many workaround ideas.
She figured the years we'd bolted from the relentless
Dog Street dogs would make us naturals, and then we'd
fit in. For a week, I'd forgotten that I hated sports and that,
if given the choice between a letter jacket or a leather one,
I'd go with the gleaming black cowhide every time.

Now, fire pursuing us, crouching in the starting position,
she gives me a face of "I Told You So" followed by a "Mark
Get Set Go" one and we charge the flames. We raise our legs
trying not to hit the burning hurdles, close our eyes, and hold
our breaths, hoping the wall of flame is not as deep as
it seems, wishing we'd each thought to invest our summer job
money in better sneakers that were more flame resistant.

Of course, because you're reading this,
you know we made it. What you don't know
is that we land only partway through the flames,
melting our soles some as we bolt blindly the rest
of the way, break through to the other side. What

you don't know is that we could have been wrong,
that we were just lucky. Streaked in smoke, we shiver
in the close call and walk home, never looking back
to see if that swamp fire liked the taste it got. What you
don't know is that after a while, shaking can seem like
laughter, if you want it to, and by the time we emerged
still trembling from the bush line and saw familiar houses,
this was what we told anyone who asked, and this is what
we also tell ourselves. We had just experienced the best
joke, but it's an inside joke, and you had to be there. We tell
ourselves this over and over but when we each get home,
we take off our shoes, see our scarred soles, and know
how close we came to losing everything our ancestors
fought for, and man, they'd be pissed when we eventually
arrived in the Skyworld, we might even get a rare slap.

But we were lucky enough that the scolding we'll get beyond
the Star Path should be years and years from now, if we just
smarten up, and I guess that's why Jaboozie has applied
for financial aid, taken the SATs, and is leaving for college
in a couple weeks, getting ready to move into a dorm, a few
miles or a few million miles from the Rez (they seem the same),
taking enough belongings to stay a good long while.

From Iron Man to Skywalker: 6. Cliffhangers and Disc Jockeys

Because I still have a steady job after school, I still blow secret
cigarette smoke out my bedroom window screens. Some
nights, I still offer the few extra dollars left from my paycheck
to my mother for BINGO fantasies, and she still accepts every
time, insisting we'll split the jackpot when she wins the coverall.

Her purse will still be as empty upon her return as it was
when I gave her the five dollars after supper, but I still
want to be home alone to watch TV or listen to music
and smoke my fool head off without skulking around,
and she still wants her friends to think she has enough
leisure money to still waste on BINGO seven nights a week,
like they do, and just like that, this has become a tradition, so
these freedoms seem reasonable enough to invest in for both of us.

But when I am seventeen, one night, a few minutes after
she walks out to wait for her ride at the end of our driveway,
I am lighting my first Marlboro Light, watching the plume
stream from my mouth into the living room, as I settle in
to watch *Magic Shadows*, a show on Canadian public
TV specializing in old-time Cliffhanger serials,
like Captain Marvel, Captain Midnight, and all
the other Captains who ruled these shows, always
getting into trouble at the last minute, so you'd have
to tune in again to see how they got out of the mistake
they'd just made: stepping on the trapdoor, attempting
to cross the sketchy rope bridge, running into the burning
building, trusting the wrong person with their safety.

As dumb, implausible, and predictable the resolution
when you came back, I always returned, worried
but secretly knowing no harm would come, that they would
always be there. When Captain America, wrapped in the flag
as he was, flickered imperiled in on this unsteady transmission
across Lake Ontario, I heard the door open, trailing a deep,
masculine cough that I knew could not be my mother, giving
up on her ride. Instead, my father walked in, peeking through
the heavy curtains we used to keep out the cold that enveloped
our front room. He mumbled a hello, as if he'd been coming
home, every day, for the last seventeen years, instead of
acting like the ghostly windy-day TV signals we tolerated
with no other choice, phasing in and out of our lives.

He'd been living in an uninsulated house down
the road, with a bunch of other Rez squatters who had
similarly wandered away from their own families
for reasons that made sense only to them. Autumn was
coming on, and I didn't think that shell of a house
had a stove or fireplace, or much in the way of furniture.

I mumbled my own greeting, and retreated to my room,
wondering what he was doing there. I put on a record,
and waited, peeking every now and then down the stairway
to the limited sight of his foot, tapping in time with my music
as he sat in the corner chair my mother usually sat in. This
surprised me, as she told me years before, he'd been struck
by lightning sitting in that very chair. Because we didn't live
in comic books or movie serials, all he got was burned
and rattled a little, and a starburst-shaped scar on his chest,
and no super powers to speak of. Perhaps he was trying anyway,
thinking his chances for metamorphosis were Best Two

Out of Three, or maybe he feared another zap, and believed
that folk wisdom, where lightning never struck the same place twice.

I changed records, stacking the spindle with Rush, Ozzy
Osbourne, and any other band whose music didn't
encourage the act of toe tapping, thinking he might get
the hint and leave, but he didn't until a few minutes
before ten, walking out so close to the time that BINGO
let out, discharging my mother and her empty purse,
that I thought they must have run into each other in the driveway.

He didn't know our woods well enough to use the paths
we'd carved, so maybe he just hid in the bush line until
she passed, standing silent, not breathing, so she might not
notice his scent, probably familiar even after all these years.

He kept this up that entire winter. Whenever she left, he'd show,
say hi, and for the next three hours, read the local newspaper
which was so empty of any real news, you could read it
front to back in less time than it took Captain America
to find himself back in trouble again. When spring came,
and I eventually told my mother of his nightly appearances,
she lit a cigarette and said, laughing, that maybe he was just
looking for a place that he might find some warmth.

Hunger Test 3. Cumulative Exam

Part A.

Because the kids just down the road
are closer to you, in experience and age,
than your siblings, you spend most
of your time with them. They feel closer
to brothers and sisters than they should.

All winter, you wait for the bus with them,
though sometimes they don't bother to go
when the bus pulls up to the driveway and waits.

All summer, you live days together in grass
patches and dirt piles, and the ghosts of cars
and basketball hoops around the houses.

You do this only five days a week, but summer is tricky.
Sometimes you forget it's Friday and you haven't retreated
before their father brings home their weekly ritual.

Friday is payday for many men on the Rez, the day
they act like they belong to white families beyond
the border, splurging as if living suburban lives,
for one night a week. In this house, the splurge
means pizza (2 full trays) and wings (family
bucket of 50), that their father brings home
with his lunch pail, where he has sometimes left
part of his dessert for his kids to plunder
and fight over, learning to be cunning, developing
skills of survival, and toughening their hearts.

On occasion, none of you hear him pull into
the driveway, so steeped are you in alternate
universes of your own imaginations, playing:
"house," "corner store," "Rez clinic,"
"charity carnival," and when no grown
ups are looking, "Indian Bar."

At these times, you look up, smelling pizza
spices and feeling the pinprick burn of wing
sauce in your sinuses, just before their father
turns to you directly and says, "Time for you
to go home," as he distributes paper plates
and Styrofoam cups on the table where you
have just spent the entire day. Do you:

      a.)   get up silently and pretend you were leaving anyway?

      b.)   slowly rise, thinking he might change
              his mind, just this once?

      c.)   tell him some made-up story about your own
              impending supper across the way?

      d.)   tell yourself some made-up story about
              what awaits you at home? (what does it include?)

      e.)   tell yourself that next Friday you will
              remember and stay away, play alone,
              listen to albums, and imagine the future?

      f.)   tell yourself that next Friday, you will
              once again, slowly rise, thinking for once

he might change his mind, and pass you
one of the cups and one of the plates?

Part B.

Some of those Fridays, you stop by
the darkening house on the family plot
before the sun sets because your uncle
there has no electricity and goes to bed
with the blue skies turning orange and
a deeper purple before fully retiring.

On those occasions, do you hope:

    a.)   he's thawed some stew beef he stored
                in your family freezer on grocery day
                (and for once would not smother it
                in the abundance of onions he ate
                because you got a lot of flavor
                for the low price of a good-sized bag)?

    b.)   he maybe has hot dogs, which keep
                in his old-fashioned icebox, chilled
                with old bleach jugs filled with cold well water?

    c.)   he won't ask you if you maybe have
                a "fin" he could borrow, because if indeed
                your pocket holds a five-dollar bill, you will
                give it to him and hope he remembers next month?

    d.)   he might share the secret of how
                he learned to live with absence,
                no electricity, no plumbing, no

insulation, no way out, no
companion, no method of stopping
this unending hunger except
his guitar and a radio, rationing
battery power and groceries and
learning how to play without
a High E after that Tuning Peg
got stripped from being cranked
too tight, one last time?

Part C.

When you get back to the house
where you belong, the only one
home is your other uncle, who has,
aside from a WWII stint in Africa,
rested his head in a tiny upstairs alcove
in the House on Dog Street.
You don't know if your mother has
not yet gotten home, having no luck
with rides, or if she has come and gone,
desiring an occasional Friday night
to call her own, instead of someone else's.
He is at the stove, boiling some small
game he either shot, himself, or received
as payment for helping someone else
on the Rez keep their home together for
at least one more tough winter on the horizon.
You know the fridge contains remaindered
bologna, a couple lonely, greasy slices, a pitcher
of instant iced tea, milk for coffee, assorted
sleeves of condiments (courtesy, the Kmart Cafe),
eggs, and some frozen stew beef and chicken

parts, targeted for Sundays or your other uncle's house.
Do you:

a.)   look in the cupboard and gamble with the shiny
label-deficient cans of commodity food, hoping
for peaches or pears, and not "Meat in
Sauce," to OPEN IN CASE OF EMERGENCY?

b.)   remember all the other game you've tried
at a series of Rib-showing Rez houses
(deer, squirrel, pheasant, grouse, rabbit)
and take your chances with your uncle
and his invitation to join him, knowing
you will need to feel the meat you chew
with your tongue, so you don't swallow
the lead pellets, or break your teeth on impact?

c.)   chug a couple of glasses of instant
iced tea, savor the powder grit on your
teeth, and head to your room, smoking
cigarettes, one after the other, suppressing
your appetite, while you fire up
the turntable, reach for the White
Album, the Beatles' singular vision and
sweet inhuman harmonies filling
your empty ears with so many
treats, "Honey Pie," "Savoy Truffle,"
bacon, "Wild Honey Pie," even
the transparent layers of a "Glass Onion,"
slicing such deep grooves as they enter,
that your stomach forgets its empty
state long enough for you to fall

asleep and dream of a time, a place
where you might have leftovers, because
there was enough prepared, for you
to have taken too much to start with?

How to Be Less Popular in High School When You Are Indian and/or Poor

1.   Waste money you do not have
on designer clothes (not knockoffs)
like the white kids in your class;
pretend you did not pay for them
with the minimum wage you receive
for scrubbing the buses they ride
to school, for scrubbing the urinals
of the mechanics who keep those buses
running reliably for their educational needs.

2.   Upon demand, compose a letter to the principal,
acknowledging that you've been told you do not
need three English classes to graduate, acknowledging
you've been told you will be at a disadvantage if you sign
up for College Prep and Advanced Composition,
given the general battered shape of your transcript so far.

3.   Rigorously study the novels of Stephen King, the lyrics
of Rush, Pink Floyd, Bowie, Beatles together, Beatles apart,
write your own similar work about authoritarian rule, isolation
and desperation, oblique and nameless love, the Monsters you
know, the Monsters you don't, and never correct people who
read this work, when they assume you are telling it truthfully
from the Monster's Point of View, that you are writing
the true story of your life.

Because you will eventually recognize this is exactly what you are doing.

From Iron Man to Skywalker: 7. Clone Wars

Likes millions of others, I find my voice through
Luke and his barren life under those twin suns
of Tatooine and all the ways he insisted his life
was going nowhere, in 1977. Three years later,
we were ready to see what he was up to. All kinds
of people got tripped up on the strange Lucas Universe
names, the way others can't even shape the sounds
we make for words in our language. But we know
all kinds of Skywalkers. More than half the men
in our communities build the iron skeletons
of skyscrapers, and they walk, proudly fearless,
those stories so high in the sky, they sometimes feel
clouds passing by them as they break for lunch, legs
dangling into nothingness as they eat incompetent
sandwiches they've made, themselves, so far from
home and their wives and children, counting the number
of stories they rise into the sky every morning,
the number of days until they can go home, even
for just a few moons at a time before they walk the skies
again to keep food on the Rez table. They tell themselves
the months will fly by, because that lie softens the ache.

But Luke had a different take. He told himself he wanted
to leave because the flickering hologram of a woman
in trouble projected itself into his deep desert hole, next
to a broken vehicle he had no means of repairing. What
really gets him to leave that lifeless place: the slaughtered
corpses of his only remembered relatives; the power
of his father's thrumming sword, finally landing
in his rightful hand; the vague stories of an old

man he'd only heard of secondhand, nicknamed
into obscurity; the promise of adventure;
the possibility he could make a difference
in the life of someone he'd never even met?

Most people forget that at the beginning, he plans
to apply to "the Academy," a direct gateway
into the Empire. Do we long to be Rebel Luke?
Do we, those who have fallen under this spell,
know what it's like to feel family are strangers
and strangers are family? Did we feel that all
our arid dreams were within reach if we were okay
walking away from everything we knew? How did we
feel, then, three years later when the Empire Struck
Back, and Luke, running away from another struggling
family, another series of broken promises, had to face
the truth? The person he believed to be the galaxy's
most relentless villain was really just his own father,
absent all those years, now showing back up, expecting
some kind of loyalty or at least a slice of obedience?

Some of us already were familiar with this kind
of story about fathers and their expectations
however unreasonable and selfish, the ones they
had for the children they'd left behind to chase
their own dreams and desires. Some of us were
not at all surprised when the Sith Lord, Darth Vader,
cuts Luke's hand off, as it held the sacred object
he'd left behind, the only link between Skywalker
father and son, in the lack of any real shared
history. We knew already from our own past
experiences that he'd do something just like

this rather than risk harm to himself that son
might have inflicted, grown so tired of imagining,
waiting, and wondering what had really happened
to his Father in the Clone Wars. Some of us knew
that if Luke were given the choice, the android
hand he later got fitted with, would be the same
make and model wired permanently into Vader's
central nervous system, like shared DNA from
a galaxy so far, far away, and not
such a long time ago . . .

Electric Blanket as Ouija Board in Sixteen Parts

1.

I listen to radio signals from Toronto, humming
across Lake Ontario into my bedroom speakers. They
suggest different places I've never seen, beyond
glimpses flickering across our TV screen. Transmissions
and radio songs are clearer at night, with less interference.

A New Wave rushes through the mesh, rippling
the hairs deep inside my ears with the sound
of unfamiliar music that demands to be heard,
just the same notes rearranged and refracted,
mysteries to be unpacked and interpreted.

These songs shifting in and out of understanding,
remind me of the occasions my mother pulls the Ouija
Board from the crawl space where we keep Christmas
ornaments, and clothes no one can remember why we saved.

2.

Demanding answers to our secret desires, we
stare at the board with its alphabet, its Sun
and Moon, its Yes and No, and at some point,
every one of my brothers and sisters rest
their fingers on the planchette,
(the little heart-
shaped table with its
circular window at its
center, like a bull's-eye).
They let it slide freely over letters
and numbers until they arrive at the words
gracing the bottom of the board: G-O-O-D

B-Y-E, their belongings already secretly
sorted into what to take,
what to leave behind.

3.

When they take its advice, and come home,
for Christmas or birthdays, they offer
our mother gifts of warmth for Christmas
and her birthday, like gloves, scarves,
boots. They know when they leave that each
person still living there, will have more trips
out in winter, to draw water from the pump,
for baths, for cooking, and drinking.

4.

Filling the water pail is a chore
you cannot deny, or leave until
your supply is almost gone. You may need
to boil water on the stove, to run into
the frozen pump mechanism. We could melt
snow to accomplish this, but our mother believes
that you should only pour water into a well
that the water had been drawn from. Maybe
she got that wisdom from the spirits
trapped by the planchette's heart.
(It seems like a long message
for unhurried spirits
to spell out, letter by letter,
but maybe the afterlife isn't
that busy a place.)

5.

They never leave gift sizes open for
interpretation, for she might give

away warmer gloves or better insulated boots
to anyone else wanting to keep the cold
out, too, often finding a way, anyhow.
One brother, in his quest, shops for presents
aware that, in his new trailer, they can nudge
up the thermostat and warm air will rush
into every room in their rectangular house
with ductwork running beneath it like
a circulatory system, their furnace humming
louder whenever they want to raise
their comfort level. He wanders
stores, knowing he can't build central
heating into our drafty house to boost
our two kerosene heaters that radiate
heat and soot into our lives and lungs,
when he discovers the perfect gift.

6.

The electric blanket, with its wires
like veins, sending heat through cloth,
will give the person beneath the covers
the illusion that they live in a warm
house for the hours they sleep. Unlike so many
other gifts, my mother accepts this without question
and throws it on her bed the night she receives
it, keeping it on, the orange bulb on its adjustment
knob serving as a night-light in her cold back bedroom.

7.

We all love it from afar, briefly lying
on top of it evenings she isn't home,

wondering what it would be like to sleep
beneath its electric hum for an entire night.

8.

None of us mention the history of Indians
and the gifts of blankets. Best to pretend
the U.S. Military did not trade blankets
covered in Smallpox knowing the Indians
wearing them would breathe the invisible
particles, that their skins would become
reptilian with disease, and they'd cough and never
stop until their last breaths prevented more.

In a drafty, hundred-year-old house, between two
Great Lakes, you get over your fear of symbolism
and history. Blankets are not an option nine months
of the year, and for a full three deep-winter
months, ice covers both sides of your windows.

9.

When I am in high school, she finds
another electric blanket. I don't even care
that it's Baby Blue, a color I hate
because it reminds me of the vulnerable
years you spend swaddled before you can walk.

It is on my bed, already plugged in
and warming, when I get home, frozen
from pumping gas after school for minimum
wage. She lets me discover it after supper
when I crash for an hour, every night trying
to thaw out from that day's endurance test.

She calls it one of the Rummage Sale Miracles,
that she keeps track of, justifying the hours
she digs through bins and boxes in church basements,
fire halls, white people's garages, and stores
like Goodwill and Salvation Army. All the other
Miracles that dot my life so far (a *Lost in Space*
Robot, a *Land of the Giants* ship, a *Wizard*
of Oz puzzle, a Batman helmet) reveal the reasons
they were abandoned by their original owners.

No one gives away a robot with both of its
arms still attached, a spaceship complete
with sliding hatch, a puzzle with all 500 pieces.

But she's been so used to divining answers,
she doesn't even need the Ouija to arrive
at justifications, all of which criticize
the previous owners as lazy. We can make a new
robot arm from tinfoil, paper clips, and clay
we didn't actually have, neatly cut a perfect door
for the ship out of cardboard, color new
pieces for the puzzle, testing our skills
at matching. Even my first pair of Levi's
when I was eleven, she insisted were broken
in perfectly, but I discovered the next day
in school that they were "donated to charity"
because the fly would not stay up. She insists
she can sew in a stronger, better one.

10.

One night, bright flashes disturb
my closed eyelids inviting sleep,

and I wait for the crackle and rumble
of thunder, even though winter has arrived
and we almost never see lightning while snow
covers our long expanse of front yard.

When it doesn't come, I open my eyes and wait,
studying the posters I've mounted on the walls, trying
to hide holes in the plaster, reducing drafts that push
in, depending on wind direction, as every brother and sister
has done, with their time spent waiting in this room.

11.

I am finally to the age where I have
the big upstairs bedroom to myself,
but only because all the others
have taken the Ouija's advice, having
already said G-O-O-D B-Y-E to our address
on Dog Street for as long
as there has been a Dog Street.

When I shift in this ancient bed that held most
of my sleeping siblings at some point, to adjust
my position beneath the posters I've ditched
theirs for, light flashes again. Those gleaming red
Rocky Horror lips whisper that I have discovered
the way this Rummage Sale Miracle is like all the others.
The lightning jumps not outside but between the blanket's
inner and outer layers, lighting soft material like
clouds during a hot summer late-night storm.

12.

The blanket's nervous system of electrical cords
is frayed, and sparks arc between broken lines

of insulation. I wake my mother and ask her what
we should do, hoping that, as in all her other
choices, she'd know of a way to salvage this Miracle.

We don't have another spare blanket
so she does the one thing I didn't want
to see, unplugging it and feeling its mass
thoroughly, pressing her own weathered
lips to it, the way she might check
your forehead for fever.

She knows better than I do that no
twelve-inch robot or plastic spaceship
ever killed anyone outside the world of
lame TV horror shows, and all our history
for generations rises up as she smooths it
back onto the bed, and tells me she'll stay
here the night, to watch it, ordering me
to sleep in her bed, instead.

She says you can never trust a blanket
that has gotten a taste of you, a taste
for you, but I tell her it's okay,
that she should go back to bed. I'm old
enough now to have figured out, I should
have just unplugged it, myself, and gone back
to sleep, dreaming of my own meager body heat.

13.

But in high school, I don't want to have all
the answers, don't want to be helping to pay
the bills each month. My only extracurriculars

in the yearbook are lies I've snuck in,
because I've never attended German Club
or the Native American Culture Club meetings,
and I surely have not tried out for any sport,
because when the bell rings, at the end
of the school day, I punch in for two hours
of work each day, and every two weeks,
the United States government takes money
out of my pay for Social Security, to be used
by me in old age, assuming I get there at some point.

14.

She goes to her own bedroom downstairs, knowing
she fell down a flight, in an earlier home fire, escaping
through the flames because it was either that or die
carrying my unborn older brother. The last home fire
we had was maybe a decade ago, when I was smaller,
even more insignificant. The hallway light fixture
leading to my mother's bedroom, shorted and burst
into flames, when someone flicked the switch to better
see what was in our overstuffed hall closet. We saw it
happen, and put it out with so little drama that no one
even bothered to see if the Ouija Board and Christmas
decorations, inches above the flames, got singed. We got
back to whatever we were doing, pretending our home had
not just tried to commit suicide, and we wondered how many
other frayed wires lurked in the walls of our patchwork
home, with their haphazard construction. After that small
fire, only one outlet and one switch still worked, and we
rewired the house with extension cords, an external
nervous system, that we could at least touch, to feel if
they were getting too hot, to feel if our house suffered a critical

fever, at any given time. Does she believe these sparks
are a premonition of the inevitable and shut her blanket off?

15.

I don't know. I check the cord one more time, making
sure it hasn't plugged itself back in to the extension
leading into my room, when I wasn't looking. It is
the middle of the night, and I touch the tips
of my thumbs and index fingers together, make
a heart-shaped gap, and run an invisible
planchette across the whole blanket, looking
for lingering sparks and embers of answers: Yes,
No, the alphabet and the ten numbers that run
into infinity in variation. The moon
will fade and the sun will rise in a few hours.

16.

In a couple of years, I will have to make the decision
my brothers and sisters have made, find those
connected letters on the board bottom, G-O-O-D
B-Y-E, and I wonder who then will check
for sparks in the late hours, when everyone
else is asleep, who will touch the extension
cord links between plug and outlet, searching
for the wrong kind of heat creeping itself up.

But this night, I am still in school, and I crawl back
beneath the blankets, tune back to the signals calling
from Toronto, whispers of a future beyond the world
I know, where houses sometimes spontaneously disappear
in sparks, smoke, and flame, leaving no traces we were ever
here. I think it will take hours to doze. But Indians are used

to defying our own dangerous history, and I drift, thinking
of the Pink Floyd pyramid on my wall, stark in the desert.
Who believed he was so important that his grave required
thousands of others leaving nothing but their own skin
and blood on those stacked blocks, while he inside gradually
disappeared? Those thick glistening red lips on the *Rocky
Horror* poster sharing space on my wall whisper that I
already know the answer about the kinds of people who
believe they deserve the sacrifices of lesser people, that I
see and interact with them every day and that I should stop
pretending, ignore the inevitable sparks of my own vanquishing
flame that will make me disappear into carbon dust, and go back to sleep.

I've got a long day ahead of school and work and if
I'm lucky, I'll return to a home still standing.

Jaboozie Passes Me the Book

Because she's moved in to our
family solar system, confirming
the love of her life two doors down,
we see each other all the time, maybe
even more than she or my cousin
would like, sometimes.

We are leaning on the car, waiting
for my cousin, getting cleaned up
after a long day roofing. His car
windows are wide open, keys in
the ignition because this is the Rez.

I notice *The Reservation* resting
on the passenger's side. And by this,
I mean the book, by Ted C. Williams.
The actual Rez never rests, but this book
lies dormant fairly often. One of my half-
assed cousins (the maybe blood-related,
maybe not kind), Ted had left the Rez
long before I was born, but came home
to visit often enough, and the summer
I was eleven, he made Rez news by
publishing this book, creating excitement
in some, and hostility in others.

At that age, the idea of reading for
pleasure had never occurred to me.
Many households around the Rez
have a copy somewhere, but I didn't

think I knew anyone who had read
the whole thing. Jaboozie is in
college and says she has enough
to read, but her man, my cousin,
is reading it, a little at a time,
maybe on his lunch break.

Two of my uncles were named fleetingly
in its two hundred pages, and I reach
into the car window, flip through pages,
to see if I can spot their names.

Of course, I'm not looking for their
legal names, since no one uses those,
but their Rez names, and I spot one,
transported back to some of the old houses
already gone, think of elders, already gone,
still alive on these pages. I keep reading
until my cousin comes out and we head
to the city seeking whatever trouble
we prowl for that particular night.

Back through our border, I ask my cousin
if I can borrow the book for a couple
of days. He says it will take longer than
that, but by sixteen, I've been reading
for pleasure maybe three years. I cover
half that night and the rest the next
evening, staying home.

I ask my mom if she remembers
an event Ted described, and she says
she remembers the truth instead.

I understand now why so many people have
this book, but so few read it. They wanted
Ted to use their mirror, but he peered in
his own, instead, and his was long and wide,
and the mercury on its back surface shone
clear, or maybe its imperfections were ones
he knew best because they were his own.
He rearranged people's lives to protect
them and celebrate them at the same
time. He was writing a history that
insiders would understand one way
and outsiders another way.

My mom didn't understand that she
wasn't the intended audience, and
that the white readers everyone worried
about didn't even exist for the most part.
The secrets revealed in those pages weren't
worth knowing, to them. The real secret,
the one waiting for me and anyone like me
in the future, was the most daring of all.

Ted held the mirror up to me, not so I could
see him, or even myself, but instead
so I could grasp our shared world,
reshaped in careful, loving words, for future
Indians neither of us could yet imagine.

Jaboozie's Sister Teaches Me About Fire

Begin here, with her skin, bare
arm, when I am seven, in her mother's kitchen
down the road from my own. She is lifting a broken
handled frypan and I see her upper arm, naked
for she has wrestled modesty to the ground,
in short sleeves, because it's summer
and she has grown accustomed to the mirror
reflection in this minimal time.

Understand the elements
disregard the rules scarring
her like a brand, which she says can be
seen through cloth anyway, cotton conforming
to the contours she normally does not acknowledge
in the company of others, because when they see
the purple and pink twists of flesh, they look
down or up or away, but I don't have that good sense
yet and I think, if I can do this for hours,
her arm will become familiar, invisible
as air, but the hours don't drift
because we are alone and together
and she finally says to stop staring,
that soon enough I will have scars of my
own, and will learn to praise the gift
that they don't cover our bodies, entirely,
and that sometimes we can forget.

And because it is light and I find myself
asking how she got it, she says this very pan gave it
to her, grease fire igniting her flesh the instant

its handle broke, bursting her skin like a storm
cloud, and the clinic doctor said she could only expose it
to air, water, keep the earth out, hoping it will heal.
I ask why they still use the pan, repaired handle offering
a second chance to strike, at best, and she returns
that you can't let fear run your life, so you accept
the aerodynamics of nature, appreciate the clear skin
you have, and know, for its finite hunger, you should thank the fire.

And so, after all
these years, with scars of my own, I do.
I give thanks to fire,
give thanks,
for fire.

Beneath the Constellations, the Smoke Moves Home

for R.C. and the next generation,
carrying on down Dog Street

Before the moon rises and
Before the hunters chase the bear and
Before the starlight dippers tip and
Before the Old Men teach and
Before the Young Men learn and
Before they both chase a ball of flames and

After the Breakfast and
After the Run through Dog Street and
After the Princess is crowned and
After the last Cornsoup bowl is scraped clean and
After the stands have closed up shop and
After we laugh with old friends

We gather to watch Smoke
Dancers anticipate the fireball
as shadows fill the grove
with lateness and urgency
and every other movement
in the wind, shifting
with the drum and the song

And this boy, like his father
before him on a lacrosse field
moves like dance is as natural
as breathing, confident
with each turn and jump
that he is taking us home

Carrying us until the next year
when our friends are older and slower
and someone new steps forward and
joins in the dance that binds us
together beneath the constellations.

Jaboozie and I Love Naked Eyes

We somehow discover early that we
can tell each other things everyone else
would laugh at, not even dramatic secrets,
just the reality that we are sensitive people
in a culture where "sensitive" is a luxury we can
not afford. We share the toughness of having
to stand in the Poor Kids Free Lunch Ticket
Line at school every day, and we both embrace
mysterious aspects of songs we love together,
two Eclectic Music Indians in a Southern Rock
and Old Country and Western Loving Rez.

She laughs nonstop and calls me Geddy
after one buzzy night when I reveal
the epic Rush lyrics I have committed
wholly to memory, and I react the same
way at a crazy smoking air guitar solo
she grinds out on her front porch, as if
it were an arena stage, making her own
fake virtuoso sounds with her mouth,
not bothering to imitate any actual song.

Together we sway deep into the goofy
groove of Electric Avenue with Eddy
Grant and shiver with mystery at Bowie's
unearthly heartbreaking echo, insisting he
would run with us, and we knew what Chrissie
Hynde meant when she claimed that she went
back to her home but her city was gone.

Often left behind, one of us always kept
a radio on somewhere, listening to whatever
new tunes the DJs in Buffalo and Toronto
selected, not daring to miss a week, for fear
that we'd lose out on some new unexpected beauty.

But we stopped everything whenever
Naked Eyes came on with "Always
Something There to Remind Me,"
both in love with the ways thunder
crashed and blended, so buried in the mix
with cymbals and tubular bells and early
synths, so that at first you weren't even
sure you heard that rolling rumble at all
until the song came back again. Thunder
is ours. We both remembered when we first began
telling each other real truths instead of jokes,
seeing each other for real in an abandoned car,
waiting for a storm to pass, eventually realizing
we hadn't even noticed the sun come out, mud
drying to dirt so that when we walked away,
rejoined our fortressed families, we wouldn't leave
prints for others to see, a map to the place we could
shrug the armor off and live in our real skins for
a little while, and not worry about mortal wounds,
have no fear of bleeding out, washing away with
the rain and leaving no trace of our real lives.

Lines Spoken to Me Through High School and, Let's Face It, Beyond

You're pretty smart . . .
You're pretty articulate . . .
You're pretty short . . .
You're pretty pale . . .
You're pretty uncoordinated . . .
You've got pretty decent grades . . .
You're pretty organized . . .
Your cheekbones aren't very high . . .
You're not that brave . . .
You're pretty hairy . . .
You're pretty scrawny . . .
You've got a good work ethic . . .
You've got a good grasp of grammar . . .
You've got a good grasp of the subjunctive case . . .

> and almost invariably, before
> I can decide whether to concede
> or debate, they can't help
> themselves and complete
> their real thought the ellipsis
> ties to like a balloon filled
> with the methane from the millions
> of us who died at hands like theirs:

"you know, for an Indian."

Migration

Eventually, you will become what's called
an "Indian writer," but weirdly, when you make
this assertion, an unlikely percentage of people
hear you say "Native American storyteller"
instead, and they expect you to reveal life
lessons for children disguised as stories
about anthropomorphic animals, so here's
a story about siblings and reservations and
the culture of returns, but just in case
you can't hear me, let me tell you a little
something about robins and their young.

While you wait to have a bed of your own
you think about the way children are supposed
to grow up and move away, like they do on TV.
For now, you are doubtful about this claim
about your siblings and their place here.
You've heard it's like what happens
with birds, that they leave the nest. Those
people who say such things must not pay attention.

Our house, in the reservation's heart,
edges the woods, and I've spent summers
walking paths that exist and some I make with
my own dragging feet in boots that used
to belong to my brother, literally acting out
that "Indian prayer," walking epic miles
in his shoes, and still not judging anything
he might have done or might do in the future.

But I've also spent summer hours perched
in our cherry trees red and black, eating
the only food at our house in near endless
supply, ignoring those bunches of rich,
gleaming cherries with holes stabbed in them,
the size of a robin's determined beak.

Still and quiet, I see my family's movements
when they think they're alone
in our crowded house. Sometimes, I peel
bark where it's been wounded (maybe by me,
climbing), studying the occasional bug trapped
in sap amber, hard and shiny on top, but so sticky
beneath, I'll need kerosene later to clean
my hands. I'll forget and stick my finger
in my mouth, and that heating
oil, a tiny thread, will slip from my
tongue to my blood, rearranging
my DNA while I sleep.

From my perch, I've studied mid-June robins,
rust-bellied parents, fly constantly back and
forth between our lawn and nests they've built
in gaps dotting our crumbling roof, high
enough to keep out predators, like our cats.

At first, milky-eyed babies stretch too-big
heads on spindly necks, and their parents disgorge
worms and insects they've already chewed into
those open mouths. I never see the parents eat
themselves at this time, bringing everything
back, and I have to wonder how they survive,
sacrificing everything for those mouths

opened wide, with no thought except
their own, sightless hunger.

They have no idea this routine
of hunger and satisfaction
will end in weeks, perhaps badly.
Eventually, the parents will stand
on the ground below, insects twitching
from their mouths, encouraging their young
to step from the nest by withholding food.

Sometimes those babies aren't ready,
feathers and senses not developed enough
to support them as they tumble through air
for the first time. I encountered one hobbling
in the tall grass behind our house and climbed
our rickety ladder to put it back in its nest,
but my cousins insist the scent of my
interference would make the parents reject it.

Weeks later, the parent runs through our deep grass,
listening and pecking, showing speckled
but otherwise nearly full-grown robins
what to do. They still chase those parents,
begging beaks open wide, showing the border
where hard tissue meets soft. I've decided
one of these is the dazed baby I'd put back
in the nest. These are Rez Robins.
They don't have the luxury of rejecting
offspring that have been influenced
by a world outside their own.

Where they go now at night
is a mystery, all too large to fit

into their home wedged into that area
where our walls settle into the earth
and our roof buckles from the weight
of too many winters. That abandoned
cup of weeds, grass, and glue
the robins conjure themselves,
has become another forgotten
part of our house, small flakes
of blue-green speckled eggshell,
the only proof anyone ever lived there.

The next summer, at seventeen, I'm getting
too old to climb cherry trees, surprised
in the ways my body no longer fits
in the Y between thick branches.

But Robins return and begin their ritual
all over again, ignoring the old
nest and starting instead, nearby.
You only ever see two adults and the young
hatched in the spring, every year. Last year's
young are somewhere else, beginning the same
story, in variation, creating a home, sacrificing
themselves for eggs, then chicks, then
fledglings. When dropped fruit rots and earth
freezes and worms bury themselves for their long
winter sleep, the Robins leave not
because it is too cold for them, but
because their food is running out.

We don't leave because hunger is
as familiar to us as seasons turning.
Our mother never suggests there is
more food, a bigger home somewhere

else. Maybe because she is raising
us in the home where she was born
when it had only two rooms, before it expanded
with newly attached rooms dragged down
the road, left by other people's heartbreak.

Though ten (and sometimes eleven) of us live
in this three-bedroom home, every time
any of us leaves, we know the chances
are decent they'll be back, like our grandfather
who was welcomed home, despite the lingering
influence of the Boarding School
he'd been sent to, assigned to molt
his Indian identity and fledge
into that other world with no idea
when, how, or if, he would return.

Apple: Skin to the Core   GANSWORTH 2019

May I Have This Dance?

1.

Explaining Reservation Romance to a white
person is like explaining scented candles
to a person with no nose. The light and
the heat can only take you so far.

2.

When you are young, you know
there are families and that new kids
arrive, but the mechanics are unclear.

On TV, various combinations of white people
go on prom dates and dinner dates and
anniversary dates, take trips on *The Love Boat*,
and every afternoon is filled with conniving people
sleeping around with as many people as possible
on the soaps. And yet, married TV couples sleep
in single beds, a nightstand between them.

On the Rez, you can't recall seeing anyone kiss
anyone else, but every now and then, one of
the three reservation churches fills, people dress
in pastel formal clothes, and TV-type weddings
happen. Kids follow, or maybe come first.

You hear that so-and-so has been hanging
around at this other house, and you know
he's interested in someone there when he
shares venison from a deer he shot in season.

3.

The Rez is divided into ever-shifting
allegiances, around extended families
and favored activities. You might hang
with a church family, a partying family,
fishers, stock car racers, traditional artists,
ceremonial white corn planters, or you might
wind up in a family where the mother and
some kids go to church and the father
and some kids have a few beers fishing.

The choice you make will affect your standing
in that family's shifting winds. Sometimes
you say "maybe I'll just stay here," when
the answer should have been "yeah, I'll go
to that," and discover the next week that you're
hunting for a new house to hang out at, a new
family to explore the future with.

4.

You never speak of this, but you
are exploring future families.

You are trying to imagine spending
your life with one of its members.

Consequently, you are trying to imagine spending
your life with all of its members at the same time.

This is how we try on our futures.

5.

It is presumed that you will find someone
among these families to marry and start
a family, or you will spend the rest
of your days with your own family,
becoming that uncle or that auntie
everyone knows will never settle down
on another strip of reservation land,
staying in place forever, living out
your life from your single bedroom.

6.

Every door is a possible entrance.
Every door is a possible exit.

7.

This is the way we have done it for generations.
We know our courtship is not like yours, not
the kind you see continually played out on TV.

Even when we look like we are doing
the same thing you are, we are really
doing our own thing in the same space
you do your thing, so you won't try
to tug us further into your world with
some other idea. Some of us master
this camouflage easier than others.

8.

My friend Warren plans to go away to
college, in another city, even, sounding
more like the white kids than anyone else

I knew from the Rez. He's walking away
from our shifting shell game of future
families and I wonder if he'll resume
his place when he finishes college.

He convinces me I should go to at least one
school dance before I graduate. In deep dark
gymnasium shadows, white guys hold girlfriends
in places they're not supposed to, swaying in
rhythm so they can claim they're dancing if caught.

Predictably, they are the ones who demand their
girlfriends look only at the floor walking
between classes, so they don't accidentally
make eye contact with another guy. We don't
demand individual loyalty because we always exist
as a group. I think it's going to be a long night,
until Warren and I arrive at a spot he knew
he'd find, having done this before.

While the white kids are groping
and hoping someone brought condoms,
the Indians do what Indians have done
forever, finding each other and organizing
ourselves in a circle, each next to people
we laugh the most with. When music starts,
we don't quite do the Round Dance we'd open
a Social with, the one that proclaims our skills
at survival, the ways we agree on a common
step, a group rhythm. Warren finds his own
overlapping friends from different Rez
families and though he's biding time, he

doesn't let on that he'll be leaving the circle,
practicing his stealth Round Dance with the
dedication he applies to everything.

Maybe I'm the only one he's told, maybe
he knows I am also not likely to find my future
in the extended circles of Rez families.
Neither one of us has explained to the other
that we can't imagine ourselves into the Rez
futures we're presented with.

I will not hunt deer for someone and no one
will hunt deer for me. None of the maps
I'm offered lead to a path I can see, and I
have no interest in being that uncle who
doesn't settle down. I want to find the right
person, but none of the Rez families believe
the path of my heart exists in their world. Our
five-mile world seems not to have that map.

For now, I am across the circle from Jeannie,
biding my own time until I can find my world
in some other future. I perform the simple
moves she taught me, over and over without
variation, as if we are performing a ceremony.

Because we are performing a ceremony.

Jaboozie Passes Me the Atlas to My Future

Jaboozie's well into college now and we don't
see each other as often as we used to.
She works in the library and I think
she's said that is her major, but how
can a building be a major? Maybe
the guidance counselor was right
when he said college wasn't for everybody
("everybody" meaning, of course, me).
She comes home some weekends, and
Friday nights are almost like they used
to be, September bonfires stretching into
November in a good year.

"I saw this at the library and thought
of you," she says, one Friday night,
revealing a big glossy book, warning me
to be careful. If I screw it up, it's her
good name I'd be tarnishing.

I ask "what good name?" and we
laugh. It's too dark in bonfire light
to read but I can see the title is *Cult
Movies*. It is a two hundred-page guide
to my developing taste.

When I was thirteen, we heard
that *Night of the Living Dead*
would be playing at the mall,
midnight only, for one weekend,
and she suggested we could each ask

our mothers for one ride, to or from.
"You gonna dream or you gonna do?"

As with so many things, she was right,
and that night, we witness the first rising
corpses that would change the landscape
of horror movies, moving them from castles
to derelict farmhouses, at the woods' edge,
just like our own sagging-roofed houses.

"I thought you could take notes
here," she says, tapping the book.
"Sometimes they show your kind
of movies at the college, and for some
you don't even have to wait for midnight."

She can see, even in this light, that all I
imagine are the ways it wouldn't work, and
before I can come up with excuses, she
reminds me of our Night with the Living Dead.

When the movie finished, we were too
Rezzy to lobby-loiter at 1:30 in the morning,
and the ushers made us wait outside. The few
remaining moviegoers acted like zombies
staggering through the barren parking lot,
grasping at each other and moaning. We knew
they weren't really flesh-devouring reanimated
corpses, but this plan seemed more and more
like a bad idea for two Rez kids under sixteen.

"Aren't you glad you asked now?" she said. She
loved the movie I'd wanted to see, particularly

the first random attack, when Barbra attempts
to apologize for her obnoxious brother, who then dies
defending her against the first attacking zombie, noting
that's the true horror, the ways we die defending love.

"We're Indians," she added when I grinned.
"A lifetime of people are going to line up to tell
us no. If you love something, you gotta find your
own way of turning that No into a Yes,
because no one's going to do it for you."

Her mother's familiar rumbling muffler
and askew headlights announced her arrival
a few minutes later, and our worries faded to
muddy shadows we cast in their bright harshness.

And now here she was, making a liar of herself
in bonfire light. "Anyway, at least now you
know which movies might be worth fighting for.
Isn't that something?" I agreed it was. The
Atlas before me let me know what was possible,
instead of dreaming in the darkness of ignorance
wondering what things might have been like.

DOG STREET

You know, you have all the old records there, if you want to reminisce.

—John Lennon

Our vessels will travel the same river, side by side, each taking its own path, neither interfering with the other as we move forward together. The space between the vessels will be considered an undisturbed peace, to be maintained and honored by both sides.

—a version of the Two Row Wampum, the original treaty agreement the Haudenosaunee made with the first Europeans they encountered in their traditional territories

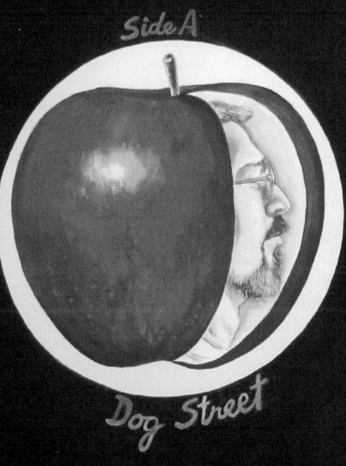

Come Together

Afternoon announcements remind us
to pick up regalia we were measured for,
weeks in advance. Velvet ropes replace
Cafeteria tables to line us up alphabetically
like our last thirteen years, but this feels more
like the Free Lunch Ticket Line, and no velvet
rope is going to invent a VIP among us.

Waiting, we're given Class Ring pamphlets
(Commemorate Your Year and Forever Friends,
Starting at $300), offered customizing options,
like Birth Stone and Mascot, for additional fees.
We may talk among friends, but NO SHOUTING,
NO SHOVING, EVEN IN HORSEPLAY!

But here I have no future jewelry.
$300 would buy my family a few
slim survival tethers. I stand
in the G–L line, with Soon
to Be Strangers. My Forever
Friends in other lines are stretched
to desperation by the alphabet's insistent
order, ignoring the clans we use to keep
track of ourselves, among ourselves.

Already, we are too far away to really
hear each other . . . without shouting.
Will our yearly rituals within Rez borders
be enough to sustain us? We will shout, laugh,
dance, and eat those foods only our own, drawing
us through our lives even with the constant snatch
and yank of the outside world pulling us apart.

Come Together

Wearing a necktie
beneath this black cap and gown.
I hope they see me
locked in this formal cloak,
trying to legitimize
lies inside my mirror
just too big to disguise.

My aunt and uncle
have flown all the way home.
Shared blood buzzes in us
harmonizing DNA
from Vegas back here to the Rez,
they've been gone for years and I now realize
they're testing the strength of genetic ties.

They know the feeling
since they both left this place.
In me they see the drive
that took them from their home,
and into the "City of Sin."
The great visit home with us was such a surprise
I don't ask them if homesickness dies.

Congratulations
come with fifty dollars
inside a card from them
as we come together
to celebrate for one final time
Dog Street family engages no polite lies.
This is their last time with our own eyes.

Something

Something lingered in summer halls, two weeks after our diplomas, while I headed to my summer job. Lockers gaped empty, cleaned, sprayed, scraped, sanitized by kid workers like me each, so no trace of us remained for September's new residents. Stickers, notes, Magic Marker hearts, and band logos are scrubbed, as abandoned as that first person you embraced in the school dance dark.

Shopping with parents, friends choose sheets, pillows, minifridges, laundry baskets, for new lives. I'd asked my guidance counselor if I could pay for the SAT in installments, like Layaway Clothes. He told me if I couldn't commit to the cost, college was not for me, that my garage labor job was the best place to imagine my future. While old classmates cooked Ramen Noodles, and declared majors, I crunched October Dog Street fallen leaves jobless and alone, past homes of folks who'd found their routines.

Wandering into a school no longer mine, I distract teachers from current students, see lockers covered in new dedications of love and lust. After everyone has gone to class, I stand in warm fall corridor light. Waves of dust spin and shine, settle in for a new year. Same old song, brand-new voices.

Not demanding that I rise or fail to meet expectations, the places I know best have no room for me. No map points me in any direction beyond Dog Street. I leave new seniors to discover their own place at the top for one year before everything they know, including their places, will be scraped from existence when they move forward, discovering whether they liked the dark, or were just waiting until their eyes adjusted.

Something

Something of the world calls out
like the moon lifting ocean waves
though I have never seen the tides

I know how the draw can be
like dismissing gravity.

City lights and their shine
on the hazy horizon glow
suggest something beyond Dog Street

but this dark and dreamless home
for most, stops the urge to roam.

On the Rez we have no leash laws
but dogs are not the cause
though the real threat of their strong jaws'
potential gives me pause.

If they didn't limit me
from exploring some of the unknown world,
beyond my own territory,

I might have chosen our ways
embraced my familiar days.

Maxwell's Silver Hammer

By November, I spend nights looking for precious metals on trash day with Benny, an older friend who works at a junkyard. He says people get fooled by shiny things and he's taped a trophy to his truck dash. This hammer gleams, mounted with an engraved plate: "To Maxwell, from the guys at the Shop, for 33 years." Benny found it next to a SOLD sign, everything Maxwell left. The Shop goes on, and one day, you're tossing the gift from your Forever Friends, because you're not there and they're not there, either.

Benny gets me a tryout at the scrapyard, separating valuable metal from the merely shiny, like Maxwell's worthless hammer. He drags objects from junk mountains and tells me to tear copper from lawn mower engines. The threads tangle and dig new fingerprints for me. At break, Benny buys me a cup from the coffee truck. I ask him where the bathroom is. He unzips, spreads his arms and pisses where he stands, saying, "This whole place is one giant toilet." In urgency, I leave blood tracks on my pants. Benny says, "You wanna keep some work undershorts, or they'll all be dotted red." I only have one pair for each day.

Weighing in, Benny grins at his three Franklins, but my eight hours yield ten dollars. Benny says, "You'll get better but nothing stops the bleeding." The next morning, as I try to touch only my fly's metal tab, he adds, "Freaks my old lady out so she buys me black ones." That night, with newly altered fingerprints, I am relieved to be the only person who sees my daily revised maps of blood.

I stick to white briefs, keeping track of how much blood I let. What did Maxwell tolerate years before he'd had enough of life with "the guys at the Shop"? How much flesh and blood needs to leak from you, leaving trace elements before you vanish from the place where you once belonged?

Maxwell's Silver Hammer

I sort heaps of trash, struggling for survival cash, spending nights alone
wading through abandoned junk and sludge, aching at the bone.
My choices are dire, warming bloody hands with fire, have no one to phone.
To ask if maybe I've lost my way, hear just dial tone
and I spend alone another day. How did I get so lost?

Old classmates have gone to college, leaving their homes in fall.
They are off seeking some knowledge, but I've been left by them all.

How did I not see, where they would be leaving me, when we crossed the stage?
They were told they'd be going away, new lives ahead.
They would find new friends, new beginnings and new ends,
grow along the way, discover what it means to have real
compromises and as they grow into their own lives
I try to cope at home.

Dreams of drawing with pen and quill, fade like a distant call,
as this life drains me of my will, and then my wherewithal.

One day in the gloom, my mom asks in my room, if I have trouble
that I might prefer to keep private. I have no clue.
She holds up my briefs, dark blood spots stand in relief
asks about the cause. (what can be the cause?)
"In the junkyard I pee, my cut hands bleed,
leave tracks behind, across my fly," I say, my face red.
"You think this works?" she asks.

"If you stay sorting junk and scrap, until snow starts to fall,
you might just as well put a cap, on college dreams at all."

197

Oh! Darling

My mom only calls me this when she wants my attention.
It works because she never lets anyone see inside her barricaded
heart like that, sending out a signal that her armor might have gaps.

"I can tell gathering your clothes for laundry day, in the ways
your bedroom grows full with emptiness, that you already think
you might change your life and that you'll have to leave this place behind."

I'd been storing belongings I wanted to keep, in boxes
beneath my bed, the way we save things we love most
in this house, leaving the rest untouched, sealed in amber,
part of me sustaining or frozen, in my old room.

"The things you're packing tell me that you still live
in a place where you believe your voice will count.
If you stay here, that voice will blur into all the others,
waiting for our ways and memories to be valued by others."

My mother says to me, her last son, words unformed
with my siblings, whom she told over and over again,
that "it's a white man's world." Does she think I'm
smarter, more ambitious than my siblings who've come
and gone and come again, or more stupid and naïve
because I shared no memories of their life in that world?

"Take only what you need now. The rest
will be here for you whenever you come to
settle in the new place you'll call home."

Oh! Darling

She sprinkled a torn tea bag
into my favorite cup
poured water and let it steep
then insisted I drink up.

With an unsteady settle
she sat down at our table
and stared into my teacup
seeing what she was able.

The futures that are swirling in my drying leaves
offer no assurances, no treasure
but she won't yet grasp that I no longer believe
her visions with any real measure.

She stopped reading for others
years before she took my cup
trying to prepare me with
the only help she could give.

Tea leaves for me belonged to a different world
when we'd loved dark shadows and mystery
damp flake picture glimpses of unclear life unfurled
instead of the new place I want to be.

"When you leave us here behind
you will likely stay on track
but accept there will be times
you'll want to find your way back."

Octopus's Garden

Every year, we climb the four-story wall to watch the sun rise at least once from on the dike top. Stars melt and reflect in morning waves. The reservation woods are skeletons stripped, sick dogs leaving home and going to ground. The first snow will fly soon, and we won't watch the sun rise or set again here, until spring. Every year, someone stops, the climb too tough, and someone new begins, finally old enough.

My cousins and I imagine creatures in the dark and glinting water, impossible in this freshwater tank built on reservation land before we were born: squid, jellyfish, sharks. We eventually claim to see the Loch Rez Monster, cruising under waves and flashes of homes, family maps; we ignore our fuzzy ghostly family story gone to water, rocks, and weeds. We have yet to learn to laugh like our parents. Our auntie's land is our imaginational generational variational. We make up the past, stealing details when our parents forgot we eavesdropped on their summer bonfire stories.

They smile and remind each other what they'd left when bulldozers arrived. We invent water monsters glimpsed on occasional nights, prowling places homes had been. Because this is our place, and will be as long as we keep that part of us awake, we will one day make love to someone, usher in a new generation, and learn to explain our own mistakes. But even now, as the sun burns off frost, I know next fall, I won't be here with my cousins, as we resurrect this warning, reacquaint ourselves with how easy it is to lose almost everything. Will anyone notice? Who will take my place? For now, we'll share our story, and walk down the barrier wall, never running, knowing gravity plays with falling bodies. We head home, morning dew shrouding our feet in the unknowable.

Octopus's Garden

It's late at night, near early light
when we climb the wall to look out on the dike.
We reach the crest and sit to rest
waiting to see what the sunrise will be like.

Together we, cousins and me,
wonder how our lives are going to be,
when we open our eyes and see
in the dark distance, our underwater hike.

Our auntie's land, where dreams were planned,
buried when the state claimed eminent domain,
we'd never seen, where she had been
when she was young and where she'd like to remain.

We couldn't grasp how she'd smile,
her old home beneath a rock pile.
We tell ourselves that we would fight
for the elders who were supposed to do right.

She had lost, at such great cost,
everything she was supposed to guard
(we are all supposed to guard).
We could strive, to keep our treaties alive,
accept our stories could get hard,
could get very hard.

Here's the deal, we never fought for real
like our moms and dads, our family.
So we could feel, self-righteous zeal,
because we never felt reality.

I Want You (She's So Heavy)

Benny's scrapyard takes more than it gives, so I weigh whether
I'd rather be hungry or cold, knowing both are headed my way.
I walk Dog Street to the west, where it ends in a T, the reservoir
blocking my way forward. The wind squeezes through rusting
street sign vents, where two arrows both point to the Rez exits.
The Signpost hums me a song to unknown places, misshapen
notes, telling me not to look back at my family home, even once.
The weight of our houses grows, years and expectations squeezing
my chest with that same vibration. My mouth and nose, the only
vents, cloud with vapor, as my lungs nearly explode.

On the table next to leftovers at home, my mom has left
a flyer someone has passed on, a jokey Indian Uncle Sam,
our confederacy belt replacing the American flag on his top hat,
an eagle feather stabbed in on the right side, in case we didn't
notice. His finger points at me, as he claims "I Want You"
(to enroll in the community college walking distance
from the Rez). I can endure five miles each way every day.
A stranger's handwritten note says they have an "Open Door,"
(no SAT needed). If one person on the Rez knows your
business, almost anyone who wants to can also have it.

The weight of this culture is oppressive at times,
behavior reported as gossip almost before you've
even finished the mischief you've discovered, but
what I want at this moment, is to find the person
whose heart has taken the interest, to help me find
the way to exhale this breath I've held for so long.

I Want You (She's So Heavy)

This new space, I've secretly sought
my own place, where I am not caught
by Dogs, tendons taut
flesh, their only thought.

I wonder how my life could be, yeah
possibly unknowing and free
become a new key
to live and to see.

In what place, would I at last land?
How could I make it all seem planned
that I'd take a stand
with a helping hand?

Who sent me the college flyer, man
Did they know my life was so dire
I felt like a liar
by holding my fire.

I turn away.
Today, I'll stay, and say, I'll pay.

I'll head away.

I walk now toward the new school
one last chance to stop being a fool
seek out some new rules
grasp a learning tool.

I turn . . .

Side B

Dog Street

Here Comes the Sun

My cousin's muffler bleats the mile
distance between his house and ours.
He dropped out of the Air Force Academy.
Between us, he was the one with promise,
support letters. Yet, he finds me six months
later, where I've been sinking in this short-day
winter, shoveling snow at night, just to get out.

When I climb in, he's breathing heavily on
the windshield and, laughing, I join him. We
penetrate the barrier, a few hundred ice crystals
at a time. In a minute he can see enough to chase
the blinding beacon rising in the east, the rest,
a blank sheet before us, glowing in the dawn.

We get stuck once, but my shoulder, only burdened
by eighteen years, gets us free as he rocks and shifts
in the rut. The car crawls on, windshield ice clearing
the same time the sky does, and when we arrive,
the parking lot looks like the driveway I shoveled
a few hours before, one thin path tracking the route
to our first day of college classes.

Here Comes the Sun

For you and I, the winter sky
reflects the new year white.

Down frozen roads, you creep to my decrepit home.
I hold my load, wait at the end of my driveway
for you to come, leave where we're from,
drive away, knuckles tight.

Getting inside, I see you shivering at the wheel.
Last year you tried to ditch this life we'd been assigned
and now we plead, willing to bleed
if we can get this right.

Seek, seek, seek, don't be weak
walk, walk, walk, still all talk
run, run, run, till you're done
breathe, breathe, breathe, vapors wreathe
go, go, go, face the snow.

Your car crawls on, windshield ice is finally clearing.
In early sun, the parking lot's hardly been touched.
To the college, seeking knowledge,
we think we have a shot.
Gather notebooks, have a quick look,
crush snow glints,
first footprints.

Because . . .

human cells elude me, I got Ds and no As for my first weeks
in Anatomy and Physiology. Missing Golgi bodies, mitochondria,
I found only the nucleus, dark essence moon of DNA and RNA.
Because I better grasped tissues, I earned a D+, knowing how
parts could pass between them. Seven generations of our culture
survived when America tried to change who we were at the core.

Because Ds would mark my exit, I needed to prove myself. For Support and
Movement, I spent hours with new friends and a box of bones, memorizing
contours and landmarks. Friends wagged fingers through the skull's oral
cavity, a lustful forked tongue. Because generations of Indian skeletons remained
trapped in museums, I could not share these jokes. Unnamed beyond "American
Indian Adult Male" or "American Indian Adolescent Female," imprisoned in
uneasy sleep, stripped of flesh and identity, harvested from graveyards, they
did not survive the boarding schools my grandparents successfully left.

Because my grandparents barely dodged the cardboard-box coffin,
I offer thanks to these bones.

Because this skull has a vertical facial bone, I know it is not indigenous.
American phrenologists insisted our sloped foreheads meant our brains
were disorganized, prone to primitive thoughts. I touch the eyeteeth,
confirm they are not "shovel scooped" like mine, a visible DNA signature.

Because my professor doesn't understand where I come from, he will
be suspicious. He does not understand every skeleton in this room, every
bone labeled across every table, could be an elder, a friend who shared food
smuggled with my grandparents, giving them an edge to survive. Because
I understand their sacrifice, I honored their help with memory, adding
to our survival story, from the D and the A.

Because

Well
Because I needed funds, I committed
words from a skull and bones.

And
Because someone gave up their bones for me,
I memorized their names,

I
took this next major test,
trying to do my best.

My professor stares in disbelief that
I could learn to study

and
earn
A
grades.

You Never Give Me Your Money

When days grow longer, announcing the future spring, my mother
and I dodge uptown potholes in another borrowed car to the sweet
spot corner of Main Street and Niagara Avenue. The Salvation
Army free parking is walking distance to Goodwill. She (and half
the Rez) imagines Lewiston rich people have donated clothes after
Christmas, used with mileage left. These stores are a roulette wheel
of possibility as they have been my whole life, but I'm interested
in the blocks between, home to a used book store where I've struck
gold, and Fever Tree, a head shop displaying overpriced Beatle bootlegs
and lurid underground comics along with their "fine smoking accessories."

Inside Goodwill, another Dog Street family efficiently scours racks. The mother,
arms bundled, says we could have ridden with her. My mother wishes them
luck, and says we are off to the bookstore. When we leave, she mumbles
that she wouldn't give that shark the five-dollar "gas money," knowing
they were already going. Instead of right, she turns left, crossing the street
so we near the Book Corner, the only retail bookstore in all of Niagara Falls.

In the window, we spot the new Stephen King, which we both knew
would be there. She says, "I suppose you need me to buy that," as if
we'd done this a hundred times before. She doesn't read much for
pleasure, a lifestyle for different people, she says, but she knows
I used to buy novels when I had a job, but can't afford them, now
that I'm a student. She doesn't have that luxury either, and I say
there's plenty of time when I'm older for the unnecessary books,
and we break the performance, head back to our borrowed car without
entering the store, ignoring the dreams it provides, the dreams it ignites.

You Never Give Me Your Money

On my financial aid forms,
we don't even exist in norms at all,
there's no "We Live at the Edge of Survival"
box to check.

You fill them in with our numbers,
I fill them out with my aspirations,
and when you ask after my inspirations
I lie now.

From the college, comes the cash,
in my hands, a sudden stash,
all this money now, one thousand bills

spread out on our table there,
thinking I won't have a care,
wonder if I have the strength and will
not to spend it all at once, a chance to still
keep warm in colder months.
Can't let this thrill make me a shill.

Roof shingling,
call the station, fill our tank with kerosene,
we'd be set for the season
seems like a very good reason to me,
canned and frozen meals would be
a taste so free for you and me (yeah, it would).
But you say, "You put it away,
if in that school you plan to stay."

Sun King

I await spring, stand
in the driveway, still
watching my breath stream
from me like memory gone
visible, slipping away,
dispersing even as I try to stop
the exchange of warm carbon
dioxide and frozen oxygen.

The sun lingers in the sky,
long enough to trickle
winter passing under my soles,
and trigger the sprouts of new year's
grass rising up through the dead
of the year just past.

When it lingers longer
on eastern farmlands,
instead of cruising low
in southern skies,
beyond power lines
and city pollution haze,
I will welcome the end
of my first furtive steps.

Sun King

In the coming spring,
my world richening,
final exams will go by,
in new summer sun will I
feel new joy living.

Jeh-oos eh awk-crhee-Awt-nes, crhee-rhoo-rhyah-kyah raw-nee-hah
Haudenosaunee Onkwehowe oo-jee-rheh-rheh raw-nee-hah-uh
Onondaga gun-naet dees-neh crhee-rhoo-rhet gun-naet roo-squat-neh-uh

Mean Mr. Mustard

Finding my own uninformed college map, I had no idea
I could study writing or painting and randomly, I choose
instead a hospital field, because most folks from the Rez
make that college choice, if they stay local like me.
I write and paint for myself, when not locked in a sterile
lab recording brainwaves and trying to imagine this divided
life will be okay—art by night, hard science by day.

But in my ward of the sleeping dead, their brains lose
grooves, and all traces of history and family. I find
an Indian man, his medicine bundle tied to his wrist,
leather tanned a yellow brown, like his drying skin.
Observing him sleeping silently through his forties, I see
how the world finds you and tells you that time runs out.

I am told he was an artist, which rattles my nineteen-year-old
world. I believed my bitter high-school job counselor,
who demanded I come up with a career plan one week,
then rejected it, and sent me back. Giving up, he asked,
if I was so smart, how come I didn't already know that
writers and artists only succeed after they've died.

I shake my comatose patient, asking if that were true, if he
had any secrets to survival as an artist, knowing he would not
answer. I was required at nineteen, to prove to his family it's time
for him to sleep, and he does for me what I could not do
for him, and what Mr. Mustard in his "advice" could not do
for me. This sleeping form, in everything he's lost, awakens me.

Mean Mr. Mustard

My coma patients cannot hear me
making my plea, to wake up again.
We're required to shake their beds,
try to stir their sleeping heads,
while kinfolk faces fill with dread,
yell loud in their ear
to see if they hear.

They never make it back this way.
They've seen their last day but I'm forced to
provide the proof their brains have died
despite the steps the doctors tried
wonder if that counselor lied
denying I had a voice
or any choice.

Polythene Pam

In July, my brother and I watch old movies and shows
recorded before we were born, from dark night until morning,
when most channels have signed off with the National
Anthem, transmitting that Indian Head Profile, in a giant
headdress trapped forever behind glass in his own lonely
reservation. We started years ago, watching *The All-Night
Show*, falling asleep as it beamed gleaming Toronto life
to our home so infested we have named mice we recognize.

He has finished college and is back home, looking
for work, playing lacrosse for three different leagues.
I ask him if he's ever been to Toronto. And he laughs
in such a way that I can't tell if he means "yes
of course," or "are you out of your fucking mind?"
I tell him I want to go there, see Sam the Record
Man, Massey Hall, Maple Leaf Gardens,
everything bright and flickering on our TV screen.

He jumps up, suddenly, swinging our flyswatter down
to the floor, where extension cords line our walls.
"You aren't going anywhere unless you actually move out
of here," he says, pursuing Pam, a mouse whose whiskers
have burned off by its chewing the cords' polythene insulation.
He chases her behind the couch he's been lying on. "She's going
to gnaw right through those live wires, ignite this house, and we'll
wake up dodging flames and eating smoke. If you want to
see anything beyond these walls, you gotta first leave
them behind before they go up in flames."

Polythene Pam

My brother comes up with mouse names
so when something happens, he'll know who to blame.
He tended to speak in code, choosing to carry the load.
I had to ask about that name.
"But why 'Pam'?"

He said in college, a girl he once knew
liked to ignite plastic and breathe in the fumes,
she'd hold all of it in, so she could feel the room spin,
her college major was her very own doom.
"No more Pam."

She Came in Through the Bathroom Window

"Anyone could break in," my mom says, pushing
an empty box through my new apartment window.

I stick my head through, to see if she's hit any neighbors,
but get stuck at the shoulders, showing her it's impossible
for even a small adult to break in through a two foot by three
foot window, and I pull back into my new living room-bedroom-
dining room-kitchen. In the bathroom she sees real plumbing
and pipes, unlike our home with pump and water pail and
outhouse, and knows that I won't likely return.

In the weeks that follow, she sends me Niagara Falls news
clippings, the "Police Blotter," tiny reports like City Crimes
CliffsNotes, with notes of her own added. She observes there's
no need to lock doors at home, in a place where anyone even
thinking about bad behavior gets turned around. If someone
tried to sell stolen "valuables," everyone would know who
really valued those objects and you'd get them back.

She says city thieves use creative points of entry, and because
I denied it, she chronically clips stories of least likely crooks and
less likely points of entry, adding stronger notes to make sure
I understand. In December, she finally admits it was only
a suggestion when she said that I should leave home. "I didn't
think you'd do it, since the rest of you have always stayed."

She Came in Through the Bathroom Window

You stepped into my first apartment
and quietly, you looked around,
fearful you'd have to fight again,
confident you could stand your ground.

This was not the life you had planned
or hoped for your final son,
choosing me to embrace our land,
sure you had picked the right one.

Standing alone with my pipes and sink,
submersing your glass in water,
you can only repeatedly think,
"Would this happen with a daughter?"

My sister had left for the city
returning in less than a year.
Brothers stayed out longer but came home,
my exodus a sincere fear.

You thought that you could change my mind,
pushing on the window screen,
sure that I would see the danger,
in my embrace of this scene.

No chance.

Golden Slumbers

Christmas Eve, a Forever Friend home from the Air Force and I linger
at my apartment. We've become adults in the year apart, and believe
our family homes will feel strange. She suggests a nightcap at a bar
that used to accept our fake IDs. There, career drinkers raise another
as we brush snow from our hair and discover our old friends have also
moved on to adult lives somewhere else. We are still the youngest here.
Underagers with fake IDs are in their parents' homes. The jukebox has
swapped our songs for this year's hits. We drink up and she takes me back.

Dog Street's familiar ruts and barking chorus join my mother
and the tiny bulbs tracing a map through her Christmas Tree
saying "I'm up," as I step into the warmth. A real one, it guides
me home with wet pine tar, needles, and well water reservoir.

She's been wondering if I'd make it. I don't have an apartment phone,
so since I've been gone, we've been hit or miss, mostly miss. We watch
the silent A Christmas Carol after midnight on a Canadian station,
preferring this "scarier version." It was also called The Right to Be
Happy. When Marley's ghost asserts itself, chains and all, my mother
whispers "we could each open a present." We look at the small pile,
and I add the few that I have brought, and walk to the tree.

For the first time I live in a place with no Christmas Tree, ornaments, or lights.
She has decorated alone, knowing we'd all be back. We resist and watch
Scrooge change his ways, then go to our separate rooms, and I reunite with movie
monsters I'd painted on my walls through high school, my other family.
For now, we coexist, she on the first floor, beneath her electric blanket.

Even separated by distance and time, together we dream.

Golden Slumbers

Before I enter the house now darkened
in my mom's driveway, hear familiar barks.
The house rests here with empty beds
inviting me to rest my head.

I've been gone for half a year,
wonder who else might be here
following the beacon clear:
This is your home, so have no fear.

Opening the door, I find there's no lock.
Almost midnight on the face of her clock.
She offered me the seat that's best,
for I have now become a guest.

Carry That Weight

Christmas over, my mom helps me pack gifts,
a warm shirt, an album of music, an album
of photos, and dinner leftovers, cut with
economy and care, wrapped in shiny foil,
lumpy treats, suggesting I can make them
last a couple meals, if I carefully plan.

She fills old shopping bags, pretending she has this
much to give, and I pretend not to notice. Back at my
place, I try on the new shirt she bought a little big, in case
I grow some more, still shopping to extend purchases over
uncertain years. The gift tag is Scotch-taped to the box, her neat
penmanship claiming a small lie: Santa had stopped at our house,
left gifts picked out just for me. Maybe he had—the scent of home
clings to the shirt like a stray piece of tape I can't pry off.

I hold the shirt close to my face and imagine her discovering
my last gift. When she was distracted by grandchildren,
I opened the fridge, left the bag of neatly saved Christmas
dinner behind, for her to find tonight, looking for
something small to eat that she thinks will not be good
enough to serve someone else. She can unwrap the slices
of turkey, the ball of stuffing, spread them on a plate and, bathed
in TV light flickering like blue flame, remember in the quiet
dark the meal we have just shared, and I imagine her tasting
that food, allowing me finally to share some of the costs.

Carry That Weight

In the city, I set my heft
on the apartment table
a bit lighter than when I left,
did for her what I'm able.

Losing my home, did what I could,
recognized her harder situation,
knowing we have different destinations,
I leave clean.

On my new shirt, I smell the smoke
of kerosene burning late,
sooty dregs from when we were broke,
gone, I can carry some weight.

The End

My forwarded mail stops
seeking me out like a retriever,
Dog Street no longer a detour,
mapping the true resting spot
of the place I'll call my own.

The only letters I get now
are those that find me in the city,
the old address where I was born
and raised, a tiny dot growing more
distant and faded on this straight line
into a future I can't anticipate, even
the tea leaves gone dry with uncertainty.

The End

In this new place
I cannot change the map, nothing left
to trace.

You and I already know here
I've lived my last Dog Street year.

Her Majesty

I see for the first time, the continent's end, breathe,
as the two of us stand on the beach, merging our
footprints from our different worlds, now together,
for the rest of our lives together, our feet immersing
in the uncertainty of futures and shifting sand from tide
washing in, pulled toward Turtle Island, this continent,
by the Grandmother your people call the Moon, that place, like so
many others, invaded, littered with discarded junk, and claimed
for the ideas and cultures of the people with enough fuel to send
a rocket beyond our sky dome, and enough firepower to ensure
they will not hear an argument when they arrive.

On Dog Street, my tiny old world remains, seven lucky miles
by five, left after the ragged bite of eminent domain. The thousand
neighbors and family members still there fire shotguns, reload, fire
again, the end of one year, the start of something new. Echoes run
through the woods I walked, growing up, but fade, seep into earth
before they reach beyond those border signs. The world outside
is impervious to those sounds, always looking to shave a few more
inches, deflect a few more memories and connections to Dog Street.

But here right now, in Daytona, stars shine
and dark waves hide the gardens of the octopus
and mysteries I have not yet even imagined. The moon
splits and divides on the horizon, grows in opposite
directions, like an embryo developing, becoming
a new life, the same story in endless variation
chasing the sky and the waves, approaching,
and we follow its path together, a new harmony.

Her Majesty

On the very last night of the year
ocean salt sinking deep in my chest
I stand with you and watch the moon here
gleam on midnight tidewater crest.

In the morning at home, I won't walk Dog Street
like I used to, collect good wishes and food
from Rez blood reasserting itself
they all smile in triumphant moods, living
together, a survivor brood.

GANSWORTH

DOG STREET TU

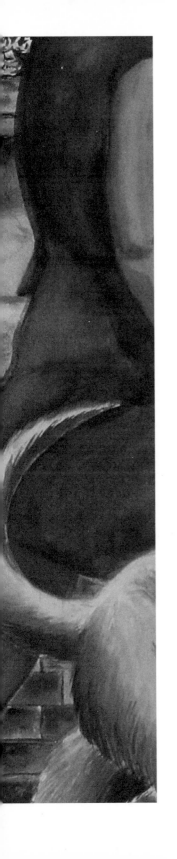

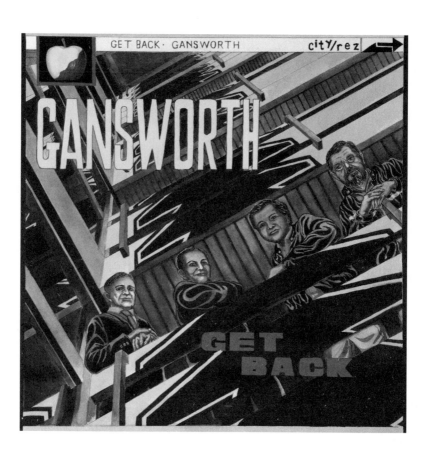

GET BACK

This is where
I once
belonged.

Peel This Skin

1.

The Human Skin is made up
of three layers: Epidermis, Dermis,
Hypodermis, and here, at the base,
legitimacy already comes into play.

You see, the Epidermis seals the body from
intrusive outside influences. The Dermis
houses scars from breaks in that seal (and
tattoo ink, if that's your thing), and its
darkness is determined by the accumulation
of melanin, the body's natural brown ink,
richer in response to environment.
The Hypodermis is said not to be
a true layer, a lying layer, as it were,
made of insulating fat and connective tissue.

The Apple Skin's color is determined by
the accumulation of anthocyanin, its natural
red ink, also richer for environmental influences,
but it does not have the same luxury as human skin—
its covering, an easily bruised and battered thin layer.

Metaphorically speaking, this weakness is perhaps why
the Apple is the fruit so often depicted as Eve's edible
error of assertiveness, her knife-keen desire for knowledge.

The Apple, tender and vulnerable, is the seat of Original
Skin. Some people grant inexplicable value or judgment

on saturation levels of either melanin or anthocyanin,
but once the skin is flayed, the insides are remarkably similar.

It's good to know some things stay the same.

2.

It is November, when I am twenty-four. Wendy
and I are in college. We met in a class
whose name I can't remember, but it was
taught by a history professor who hated history
texts, a history professor with a secret life
as a literature professor, using classic novels
to teach us 20th century history, including,
naturally, *Animal Farm*. Predictable, but neither
of us has read it because we both went to boonie
schools low on college prep, lower in academic
opportunities (though both schools were athletically
supported well—resources neither of us desired or used).

3.

Of the books I'd been assigned in high school, I remember
three: A *Tale of Two Cities*, *Splinter of the Mind's Eye*,
and *The Metamorphosis*, one for each year (my tenth grade
English teacher, on the brink of retirement and bitter exhaustion,
agreed to leave us alone if we extended him the same courtesy).

From the first of these three books, I learned
the rich exploit the poor (Okay, I already knew
that, so, really: nothing). From the second, I learned
Vader, Luke, and Leia were more interesting onscreen
than on the page (Okay, loving that far away, long ago
place, I'd read the novelization, so I already knew that,

too). And from the third, I learned that you might find
yourself transformed and exposed one day, inexplicably,
and that others will still find you undesirable, maybe
even more than you'd felt before (Okay, I'd already gone
from the small Rez elementary school to the giant white
middle school, so yeah, I already knew that last one too).

I wonder what the tenth grade book might have had
to offer, if we'd been assigned one: another lesson
already learned or another new way to understand
your place in the world you lived in? Sometimes,
it's easier when you at least know people think
you're a "monstrous vermin" that should be left
unspeakable and unspeaking, clicking and hissing
away in your bed, desperate for those in your life
to understand the ideas you're trying to reach them with.

4.

Wendy and I walk across quads, a couple
hours before our evening class starts. The only
light is a strip of burnt orange clouds, a median
dividing the darkened highway of land and sky.
Dusk often finds us here together, for this hour.
The air is cold enough to make our breath visible,
ectoplasm ghosts, but we know what awaits us
on the western edge of campus. Our destination
is an exhaust vent the approximate square footage
of the small precarious, drafty houses we were raised in.

We don't know where the warm air is being
pushed from, perhaps every heater and every

furnace of every building and every class
room and every dorm room and every lab
and every meeting room and every office
and every space claimed by others, but for
the hour of Monday sunsets before the snow
falls, this particular warmth is ours, alone.

No one can see us, when we climb the half wall
into the obscured vent, and stretch out, lie
suspended across the grate, our belongings
secured in backpacks so we don't lose
anything to muddy sooty shadows and air
shafts into the school's physical plant.
We come here when we long for food
we can't articulate. Mostly we are silent
because this roaring heat joyously blasting
on us drowns out our voices unless we shout.
We watch the horizon disappear and stars try
to penetrate Buffalo's dense light pollution and
denser regular pollution until we can't stand the cold
air dropping on us from November's crystalline
sky beyond the limited powers of our HVAC deity.

5.

Sometimes, we play a game, telling secrets no
one else knows, each assured the other can
not hear anything beyond hissed consonants
and mumbled vowels. (Though of course I know
I can hear hers and of course she knows she can
hear mine, and maybe even some other students
walking anonymously near us, hear these disembodied
confessions float by them, allowing us our privacy.)

We know the danger of this game, having both
made the mistake of playing a similar game with
our other friends, in which you tell three terrible
stories about yourself, but two of them are lies.
Your friends have to figure out the true one.

It's like that Meat Loaf song, but when you think
of that title, "Two Out of Three Ain't Bad,"
what you really mean to say here, is:
"One of These Three Is Awful."

You can only play this game with people
who really love you, or people you are
never, not ever, going to see again, people
who maybe don't even know your name.

6.
This activity is all fun and games until you tell them
* **** *** *** ** * ***** ** ********
and then they will never, not ever, see you
the same again, because after that they know
*** *** *** *** *** **** *** *** ** *
***** ** ********* and they know what
a crafty façade you've rendered, to be allowed
in their presence. You're lucky Wendy has her own
sequence of asterisks. She recognizes that no one
who has ever heard them can unlearn them
and she knows more than most what it is like
to rise up and unflinchingly be exposed.

7.
She is sometimes a model for Life Drawing
students, and I ask her how she can stand

before twenty strangers with all of her clothes
off, knowing they will not only be staring at her
for three hours straight, but also memorizing her
body's contours, mapping different shaded parts,
the scarred parts, the perfect parts, on sheets
of smudgy paper they will take with them
forever, maybe later, in seclusion, doing
things she does not desire for her image.

When we have this conversation, I've been
painting for years, but all of my models
are invented from vapor as transient as
our ghost breath on these cold November
nights. She says she knows, noting that
the breasts I draw are like none that have ever
existed on any real woman in human history.

8.

Before we graduate, she hands me a gift, a nude
photo of her taken by our friend Nate for his
photo studio class. He made only three copies
before destroying the negative. Her payment
for modeling was print number 3/3. By this time,
I've been writing a lot about reservation life,
and being in love and my partner Larry, who is not
the right age, or the right class or the right race or
the right gender. She says that, between the two
of us, I am by far engaging in the riskier act. She
says that when she takes off her clothes for artists
and viewers, it's just skin she exposes, the body's
first defense, as she makes her contribution to the art
world. At the end of the three hour session, she
can put her clothes back on and leave the scene.

9.

A month later, I understand one part of her
observation. Our friend Nate, who took
the photograph, has a painting commission
but needs a nude male reference with a small waist
and broad shoulders and, desperate, asks me
to trade sessions. If I model for him now, he will
later reveal himself and pose for me when I need it.

I have never done this but our friendship has
endured for years and I've recently come to see
the usefulness of life drawing, the value of truth.

His studio is an illegal space he and three
other painters rent above a machine shop.
While his studio mates leave, and sparks fly
and acetylene torch trails fill the air below us,
I fully disrobe and stand frozen, as instructed:
arms outstretched, neck extended, looking
at the network of wires and pipes crossing
his ceiling. I take very few breaks as it is
tough to get back into position after relaxing,
and frankly, it never feels normal to make small
talk, even with a friend, while you are naked.

Maintaining the pose, I discover Wendy has told me
the truth. I forget after a while that I am standing
wholly naked in the sun, as someone stares at me for
long periods, sometimes stepping close enough for me
to feel exhaled breath, inches away, to capture a contour,
the play of light and shadow on muscle, bone, and hair.

I study an enormous pair of metal eagle wings hanging
in the corner, like one of Bruce Wayne's or Leonardo

da Vinci's experiments. Nate has welded and riveted
them together from cut sheets of brass, individual
feathers layered and fastened in place. He tells me
the commission is for a life-sized naked angel, half
painting/half sculpture. When he finishes capturing me
on this sheet of plywood, he will cut my body loose, reinforce
my backing, and mount my wings. He says I will hang
suspended in a cathedral ceiling entryway, featured in
my own spotlight at the mansion of some wealthy Buffalo
man, presumably, until he grows bored of my body,
exposed in all its major scars, and minor perfections.

I tell Nate I'm not sure how I feel about that future,
and he says it's a little too late for modesty, and I can
tell by the region of plywood he's working, that he is
capturing my equipment in oil paint, linseed medium,
and brush strokes, and he promises to make me look good,
to put me in a flattering light, even as I express my reluctance.

10.

Two weeks later, Nate is gone, having used
his commission to support a move to the west
coast, and I have never seen him again, clothed
or naked, and I have never seen the finished work.

Somewhere, in some fancy foyer in Buffalo,
floats a young wooden Indian man, made of pressed
ply, layer upon layer, thinner than I am now, harboring
considerably fewer scars. He wears the wrong arrangement
of eagle feathers, for a young Indian man. I try not to think
often about this person I used to resemble. Sometimes

years pass before I'm again reminded of the way Nate talked
me into being exposed and captured and the way he then skipped
town, ducking on his promise to take the same risk for me.

11.

Wendy's words rise more and more often, the secrets
we told each other buried in the roar of heat we could
never get enough of. She hangs on my wall to this day
in that photo Nate had titled "Lot's Wife." My family notices
the nude woman, in stark black and white exposure on emulsion,
in the middle of an abandoned factory, only they don't perceive her
as nude. To them, she is *naaaay-kid* and it is against the way we live
to ask about such a thing, and instead, they silently honor my choices.

Wendy is right about the risks of writing, and as I have
this thought, I recall that at the end of *The Metamorphosis*,
the transformed "monstrous vermin" dies because his family
can no longer repress their repulsion. His father lodges
a piece of fruit deep into his back, where he can not reach,
and he gives up, owning the infection and starvation together
until he withers away and is quietly swept out of the house.

The rotting betrayal wedged into his back is an apple.

12.

The skin's outer layer is supposed to protect the body from
outside violations, but every guard has limits. Has my likeness,
suspended somewhere in a Buffalo neighborhood I could never
afford to live in, fared any better? Does he like his role, as frozen
heavenly figure from some other culture's beliefs, Gabriel or Icarus?
I hope at least, that this younger me faces westward so he can see
the occasional sunset and, through Buffalo's light pollution and

pollution pollution, some constellations, a few stories made of stars,
floating in sequence against the universe's unknown blackness.
His skin has maybe faded and chipped, and become weathered
and scarred like my own, from a botched surgery and the indignities
I've accrued as my years on this Earth slide and stretch into decades.

Or maybe he has protected himself better than I have.
Maybe, his arms outstretched, he has never done what
I am doing here, he has never revealed ✳ ✳✳✳✳ ✳✳✳ ✳✳✳
✳✳ ✳ ✳✳✳✳✳ ✳✳ ✳✳✳✳✳✳✳✳ and he keeps his secrets,
knowing that one thing I never learned, despite being
told by multiple people over and over again.

You can only play this game with people who really
love you, or people you are never, not ever, going
to see again, people who maybe don't even know your name.

Even then, these people must not ever know you
really can't fly, they can't be told the wings are weights,
when you leap off the cliff, and they can't know that
after the fall, you'll be left with everything irretrievably
exposed. Even if you are careful, someone may raise
a knife-sharp curiosity, break the tender membrane,
tinted with melanin or anthocyanin. Despite your best
efforts to be tough, impermeable and impenetrable,
in the end, they will successfully peel this skin.

It is good to know some things stay the same.

Indian Love Call

1.

My mother loved the songs from her youth
as most of us do. I suppose somewhere, some
day, mostly immobile elders will remember
Twerking and Electric Sliding with fondness
and their children and grandchildren will shrug
in befuddlement about their taste. But though she had
perfect pitch herself, and admired the talents of
Jeanette MacDonald, my mother refused to sing
Jeanette's most famous American song standard:
"Indian Love Call," even when a man was willing to
join and sing the part of this duet written for the male voice.

This song is from one of the musicals my mother loved
so much, from young life to the end, but in this
case, she closed the covers on the Great American
Songbook. In the movie, Jeanette and her leading
man are sitting lakeside, making lovey-dovey
eyes at each other. She is a settler woman, and
he is a Mountie, or more formally, a Royal
Canadian Mounted Policeman, or less formally,
a Dudley Do-Right. They hear a haunting call echo
across the lake, something not quite a loon, maybe
resembling human but otherworldly, uncanny.

Jeanette asks what it is, when they hear a similar
response shimmer on the lake's waves from the opposite
side, and her potential lover says, "Just an Indian,"
as he contemplates his next move, planning out how
he gets to second, third, and home base in a family movie.

For these two, and for the history of Hollywood, we remain
props, segues, or obstacles to the hero's next conquest.

2.

At one of the big family parties, my niece
leans across the kitchen pass-through, and
asks my mother, eternally at the stove, what
the Indian word for "love" is. She says "Indian"
but she means Tuscarora even though we are
Onondaga. We are here among the Tuscarora
maybe because two hundred years ago, two
people unexpectedly began to love one
another, and isn't this always the way?

This is probably one of my mother's birthdays,
where after a couple hours of too much laughing,
too many sly and coded dirty jokes at the long, hard
wood table, she retreats to her bedroom to smoke
the endless Kools we disapprove of, and watch game
shows where white people answer moronic questions,
waste money on vowels when they clearly know the
consonants, hoping no one will notice that she's vanished
like an old-time Magician's Assistant, floating in some
void until called back with the Magic Words and a flourish.

My mother claims no such word exists, insisting that
when we were still making new words in the language,
when a majority were still fluent speakers, we had no
use for such a concept. Families arranged for this young
person to marry this other young person based on what
the family of each could bring to the table, based
on what was gained, what was lost, making sure

that you didn't wind up with someone of the same
clan, preserving the future, as if nine clans across a
thousand people was a sufficient number of options
to avoid this complication. We are genealogists'
nightmares until they understand this dynamic.

When a man marries, he loses his family and
the children he and his wife send out into
the world will carry only her identity. When
a woman marries, her family takes in the burden
of another mouth and a hope that he will do his
part to contribute to the survival of all, into
the next generation and those arriving later.

My mother pretends she isn't a fluent speaker
but we know different when she corrects
us, and I realize she's decided Love was a concept
we had gotten lost with. Being an outsider,
she married an enrolled Tuscarora man who
was himself not fully Tuscarora, if truth be
told. We have been a family of lovers from
the beginning, and you only need to look
as far as our last name, and its origins.

3.

Johannes Gansevoort, born to an influential
Dutch family outside Albany, will become
notorious. His (my) cousin, Herman Melville
will go on to fame, writing *Moby-Dick*, the
Great American Novel, and will also die near
poverty, his books mostly unread in his lifetime,
but Johannes will mostly be known for the way he

disappeared: he chose love, of all things, written
entirely out of his family inheritance because
the place he found that love was Among
the Indians. A footnote to Melville's biography,
Johannes, a widower, ditched his kids to a spinster
sister and ran off with an Indian woman, eventually
settling here, where I now live, having a new set
of children, Indians disinclined to wander. He may
be buried on the upper mountain in one of those
graves whose stones have eroded so much
the names appear like bird tracks in January snow.

4.

Because my father was an iron worker, raising
stories in different cities, my parents rarely lived
together for any extended length of time. Did
my mother curse the wanderlust of my ancestor
or appreciate the freedom it afforded, so she could
raise their children in the manner she saw fit?
In some ways, she thought it was a lucky break.
She told me once, but only once, that during their
courtship years, they spent a Saturday night in the city,
socializing with her factory coworkers, and as they
walked to their car, he asked why most of her friends
were such ugly white women. She let the story
linger in the air, so we could each silently consider
why he would be interested in the relative attractiveness
of the young single women they spent time with.

5.

We have tended to embrace our family
trend and follow our own hearts

instead of trying to leverage clan
alliances for power. We know it
is pointless to seek power when
you are an outsider. All you do
when you are visible is map ways
for yourself to be harmed by others,
to give them the tools and strategies.
We are free to love who we please
even if, or maybe because, the language
we are forgetting has already lost
that word, if it ever had one.

6.

My Tuscarora-English/English-
Tuscarora Dictionary has four entries
for "love": love; love of something not
human; lover; lovesick; and one for "lust."
I am familiar with about thirty percent
of the words in my dictionary, and a few
more that some editor decided were too
vulgar to include, as if sex did not exist
because you refuse to name it.

In my thirty-ish percent of words, I have
never heard any of these Love variations,
but by the age of five, you know the word
for "bird" is very close to an anatomical word
you would not say in polite company, so you
had better learn your vowels better than
Ms. White, that blonde on *Wheel of Fortune*.
You don't want to be considered a lower
class person given to speaking those words

best shared only between two people
in a relationship, two people who
love each other, even if they can't
pronounce the actual word itself.

7.

Which brings us to you and me,
my Bumblebee (Roo (t) ter her-oo Hoo).
As with so many other aspects
of the world, there is nothing in the
Tuscarora-English dictionary to describe us,
apparently another vulgarity, another
concept you don't mention in polite
company. Though numerous cousins
have fallen in love with people who have
no tribal affiliation, or people who are just
plain white, none have made the decision
we have, to be ourselves, but we both know
that as time goes on, and we will clearly stay
together, there is no place on the Rez for us.

Tuscarora people continued to be inventive
with language even as the numbers of fluent
speakers dwindled to single digits. They developed
words for "monkey" and "elephant," surely only seen
after America imprisoned animals from other
continents and toured them around the country.
I believe the Tuscarora word for "elephant" means,
loosely, "it has a long nose," and the word
for "monkey" is "it eats lice," or maybe I have
misremembered those definitions. Maybe
the word for "elephant" means "it would stomp

you if it got loose," and the word for "monkey"
means "it throws shit at you for jailing it."

When Indians first saw zoos and circuses, did they realize
how similar they were to the Wild West Shows many
Indians turned to, in order to survive? Did those Indians
find a word for Love among their troupes? Or did they give
up and invent a brand-new one for their new worlds?

But you and I find each other and know
we will stay together in a world that doesn't
especially approve of us and the ways we love,
and maybe when my mother claimed
there was no word for love, she was
really saying that no word could encompass
all the different ways we find it.

We know the unpredictable ways
two people meet and know they want
to grow together and grow old together
even if there is no neat definition to look
up in the parallel dictionary, no map
charted to the new world they discover
together, a patch of land not to conquer
and change, or slash and burn, but instead
one to grow into naturally, over a lifetime.

Are These Tricks or Are These Treats?

After a few months, I almost grow
comfortable with carrying keys and
double-checking my apartment door lock.

I'm positive I've been gone long
enough so my mother will stop believing
I'll show back up, in the bed of someone's pickup, pushed against the tailgate by two baskets of
clothes: concert T-shirts, three pairs of Levi's,
a week's worth of briefs and socks, and my personal
junk—record crates, paintings stacked like impractical
Tarot cards, rearranging my future in a careless
shuffle, posters re-rolled in a mailing tube, my easel,
a few miniature spaceships destined for other
places, and my grandmother's sewing table, loaded
with the brushes and paints mapping my dreams.

Sure it is finally safe for a surprise
visit from the Dog Street Refugee, I am
dropped off at the road by a friend
heading east to raid his parents'
fridge in a suburb wealthy enough
to separate new money from old.

It's mid-October and though the sun
washes the driveway stones in gold or iron pyrite,
the apple tree I used to climb has begun
to change its colors, let its undernourished
fruit drop to the ground for bees and bugs
that crawl, and one by one, give up its leaves

for another year, revealing its rough, arthritic
looking skeleton hidden for these months
by the tree's sad attempts to propagate.

Beyond the house, something
is wrong with the black walnut that has
grown with me, surpassing my meager
height by the time I stop growing.
It seems impossibly moved, just
a few yards southeast, defying nature,
I think, until I realize the truth
so unimaginable, my mind chooses inventive
landscaping as the answer instead of the truth.

The entire southern end of the house
is gone, wiped clean away, as if one
of H. G. Wells's Martian warships had visited
Dog Street, pointing its throbbing cyclops
eye at our kitchen and the back storage room,
vaporizing them in a hail of animated
red optical-effect laser beams, on its way
to attempting world domination, as if
we wouldn't recognize scorched earth tactics.

As my eyes focus on absence, every missing
board, window, support beam, skewed floor plank,
across the driveway, my cousins have been
watching, waiting for this moment I would return.
One emerges from their house, left hand
awkwardly behind his back. He tells me
my mom had it done a week before, the backhoe
from a Dead Man's Road family business

showing up and driving straight through the ancient
brittle structure reduced to kindling and artifacts.
The two missing rooms were the original
tandem-room house my grandparents built after
my grandfather made it back to raise their six
children in, hoping it would grow.

"I rescued this for you, though," my cousin says.
"I yelled for them to stop when I saw the flash
of bright blue, like lightning, the familiar pointed ears."
He reveals a plastic Batman helmet I couldn't
find when I'd left, but I hadn't tried hard. Even
as a mask, it was never of practical use. For years
it was too big for my kid head, and by the time my fat
(and decidedly not "high") cheekbones fit the cowl
opening, I'd grown a beard and had to wear glasses that
would never navigate the sharply defined eyeholes
even a minimally competent crime fighter would need.

"I cleaned it good," he adds, "so it's ready
to wear. Now that you live in the city, it's possible
you could maybe see the Bat-Signal and be prepared."
The helmet had somehow wound up stored
in our back room, where we kept possessions
we no longer used but couldn't bear to abandon.
I never found out how it had been relocated, only
thankful it had been rescued and saved.

When I enter the house, my mother has
performed some kind of experimental house
surgery, grafting necessary parts of the amputated
kitchen into other areas of the house.

She's cooking at the stove now crouching
in the dining room corner where we'd
always kept a spare bed, in case anyone
needed to come home for a few days.

She then tells me the kitchen had been falling
apart, echoing what I had told her when
I'd left. "Now," she says, "when you get
back home, here, it will be easier for you
to learn how to cook." She refuses to see
I've already begun learning, looking at
the Bat-Helmet on the table, wondering
how it survived her purge, knowing
it would disappear, begin a new existence
in the city, a part of my growing life there.

After supper, I get my brother to agree
to take me back to my place in the city.
I've gathered a bag of a few more belongings,
no longer confident they will still be
there if I come back to look for them when
I eventually have more room, a stable place.

When we are in the driveway, she comes
out, warning me not to wear the Batman
cowl anywhere beyond the confines of my
own, locked apartment door. At first I think
she's teasing.

"I'm serious," she says, as my brother keys
the ignition. "Around here, you might be
Batman, but in the city, you're just

an Indian trying to hide your face
in a public place. I don't care how close
it is to Halloween, you put that on
and go to a store, the only crime you're
going to fight will be the charges pressed
against you for suspicious activity."

I don't bother to ask what activity
she means, since I've been followed
around in stores often enough, for
Browsing with Too Much Melanin,
already picturing my apartment shelf
where the helmet will perch and remain
as I assure her and wave in the rearview mirror.

Legacy

Nearly ten years after the fire that took my family
home, my cousin "Shears" routinely goes back
from his home in the city to the reservation
and mows the front lawn as he does for
the house two doors down, where his father
died even more years before. I am in my thirties
and he is in his fifties, so we each accept
that our own complex histories make
our life choices mysterious and opaque
to others, even those who share blood
with us, maybe especially those who do.

Our lawn stretched epically, the house
far from the road, hidden from prying
eyes, my mother used to say.
My grandfather Umps—the jealous sort—
once he married, made the investment,
decided Big Umma's return
gaze was for his stern face alone.

After they died and were planted
next to one another forever the lawn
became a neighborhood football field.
Though I never played, too small
and disinclined, it served to bruise
and break bones and absorb blood
of nearly half the reservation
boys of my generation.

My cousin, to my recollection, never played
football on it, was grown and married

before the trend, but these days, the lawn looks
better than it ever did when we lived there.

"He used to live with us, spent his first
five years there, got his name on that front
lawn. One day when he was about four,
he was too quiet, and you know what it means
when kids go silent, so I went to check.
He had stabbed a whole batch of fresh
kittens right through their hearts
with my sewing shears. Umps made
him leave the stains until grass grew
and spread, fading the mark and only then,
let your uncle cut it," my mother says,
by way of explanation, when I ask
what the drive is, why he cuts
and cuts the wildness surrounding
the remains of a house largely
gone back to ground.

Everybody Knows

Years later, driving behind the Rez bus, pausing
with its frequent stops, I watch the seats fill
with reluctant faces and see Lumpo's kids. I think of
him, when we are impossibly young freshmen, chewing
on Sweet Flag root, offering "Indian Medicine" to anyone
willing to listen. Some juniors and seniors laugh at his
claim because we all know how and where to find
this plant, what to do or who to ask in the way of prep,
and that it works best for an upset stomach,
heartburn, which for some people is code for
"hangover." Lumpo lives near the border, within
sight of the green sign defining the spot where
our world ends, the wider one begins, stretching
out beyond us, as far as we can see.

How casually we dismissed the possibility,
because we each shared this bit of knowledge,
instead plotting what party we might crash
over the weekend, gossiping about who was
caught making out with whom in the woods during
the last one, anything other than the medicine
offer and recipe we could ask any old person
at any random time and get the answer we need.

The summer I put my hand through a window, I
walked around for a week wincing, awakening
the tiny shards still embedded in my thumb
any time I tried to pick anything up with
even the lightest grip, before finally saying
yes to my mother's offer. We walked a few steps

259

into the woods, found a basswood tree, and she
cut a few inches from the bark and flesh, preparing
the scraps she gathered on our stove, in one
of the pans she cooked supper in every day.

She wrapped the hot, wet wood pulp in paper towels
on my hand, and I felt movement, release, for
the next half hour. And when the tingling stopped,
she removed the dressing, and tiny constellations
gleamed against the wet wood, all shards somehow
pulled from deep inside my hand, leaving me only
thin scars as a reminder, changing the roads
of my fingerprints from that point on.

But right now, neither Lumpo or I have
need for hangover cures. He's an iron worker,
like his father and my father. He helped dig through
the wreckage of the Twin Towers and I record the kinds
of lives we've lived, each keeping a different Rez tradition
alive in our own ways. We mostly see each other
at funerals and community gatherings that have
been in place for over 150 years before we were
born and that we believe will keep going long
after we've been planted on the upper mountain
someday, in the far periphery rows where they
line up those of us not legally Tuscarora.

I don't know if he can still find Sweet Flag, but
I have to pass by every window with caution, now
act more carefully in life, aware that catastrophe
can leap out at you with no warning whatsoever.
Right now, I wouldn't know what basswood or

Sweet Flag root looks like, or how to prepare them
anyway, even if I needed them and was astute
enough to remember what to do and it doesn't matter
that I remember who to ask, because almost everyone
I knew who had the answers is now gone, returned
to the Skyworld or Heaven or wherever they finally
headed to. I suspect as the years went on, they stopped
waiting for us to ask, and maybe told themselves this
was because we had somehow learned, even with
the meager lessons we'd gotten, before they left us
behind here, our confidence and cockiness knocked
fully out of us just a little too late to be undone.

Poem to the Beams in My Uncle's House, Empty These Days

Before he died, did you memorize
those rusty songs my uncle played
through brittle strings digging deep
grooves in fingers praying they would
hold out for one more chorus of "Jambalaya,"
so we could say goodbye to Joe one last
righteous time on that guitar he claimed to have
jammed with Hank Williams on,
glimpsing blues in that white
boy shucking and grinning, forgiving
him the cowboy hat long
enough to absorb that magic, steal
it back for Robert Johnson and anyone
else whose fingers bled with that
thick rich indigo liquid and infuse
it with that old Indian
smoke, sliding red into
those blues, blooming rich
purple clouds through
the greasy sound hole where decades
of beer sweat sweetened those darker tones?

We still need to sing the blues
but in the intervening years
we have forgotten the chords
that would take us home, so
if you did commit them
to memory, even a couple,
could you pass them on?

My Mother Delivers a Quick Lesson in Survival and History

The other day I was
talking about my uncle
and his house
with fondness to her—
a mistake, I know—
and she lit a cigarette
because I disapprove,
blew darkened air out,
surrounding us and said,
"I never went there, you know
that, and you should not have
either. He only smiled
for you kids because years before
you were born, he threatened
the older kids when I wouldn't
do something for him,
and I took that baseball
bat the boys had and beat
him to the point that he could not
walk for a week after, and no matter
what, he knew what was
an arm's length away
for the rest of his life."

Domestic Rate, Carlisle, PA, or
A Grandmother Corresponds with
Her Service-Bound Grandson

"I have known loneliness of the sort you are feeling now," Little Umma wrote to my brother during his stint in the Air Force at a base in Clovis, New Mexico, walking the barren stretch of plains wondering if this was the right choice to avoid Vietnam, on bad days, certain of it, most of the time. He said she sent him letters nearly every week of his two-year hitch, in Japan and then Clovis, always lifelines of endurance filled with bridges to past and future.

"My parents had my best interests in mind, sending me away as a little girl, so I would become better acquainted with the white world," she wrote. "It was not exactly the life I had hoped for, myself, but we do things we have to, keeping ourselves as alive and intact as we can. This vocabulary I have, I can trace to the school. Any time I spoke the way we do at home, I was reduced in merit points. Only the most articulate among us qualified to participate in the Outing Program, where we were allowed to be servants for wealthy white families. They told us the opportunity to be exposed to culture was valuable. You see, they wanted us to be able to speak in the presence of our employers' guests and not be the burden of embarrassment. I learned, because I wanted to make money for postal stamps, that I might keep in contact with people from home. And so you see, as I write to you, I have known the loneliness of the sort you are feeling now."

Through much of my life, I picture a tiny woman sharing a small room in my aunt's house with an upright piano, an organ, before her daughter eventually put her in a nursing home. On the occasions my aunt would check her out, like a library book, bring her back to the reservation for a few hours every now and then, she would reluctantly pull into our driveway. Though my grandmother didn't remember us per se, she remembered that she should have. She would sit in the Buick, door open, ask about my grades, because I was obviously school age, and then she would ask me if I liked her dress, explaining that her mother had given it to her, for the train ride to Carlisle, but my aunt would stop her, interrupting, correcting, assuring me and my grandmother of the facts, as if she were giving us a history lesson.

She would provide, as evidence, a reality check, "Mother," she'd say, "you know that's not true. Your mother's been dead for so long any dress she gave you would be tatters now," closing this book on me, putting it on a shelf I could not reach. Little Umma would stop speaking about her time at Colonel Pratt's school. Her training worked so well, small fragments of her reedy voice, telling me aborted stories—these fleeting sounds and observations are all I have.

My siblings, with their years' long lead, have stories, exchanges left to my imagination. It is from one of them that I first hear of her talents with cornhusk dolls and beadwork, culture she sewed and wove inside her head and heart as she was forced to learn the life of maid, cook, servant, in Pennsylvania. She was so well known for her art, I even find, years later, the article in a newspaper archive about her and her dolls.

My brother these days, driving south for vacations, his wife hating the unnatural act of flying, chooses to find Carlisle, and tells me something I already know. Left behind are some buildings and a small plaque inside an operational military institution, and he, having lived that life, is certain that no means no, when the officer on gate duty says it would be a security breach, and no amount of history is going to change that fact enough to allow him entrance. He can see it from the gate, the dull bronze, glowing mellow in the setting sun, but it is too far away for him to read what it says.

I don't tell him that about a year ago, a white scholar, like many white scholars of Indian cultures, blond and blue-eyed, of sincere professional goals, told me she went to Carlisle, asked the same question he asked, and was allowed in, with a group of students, no security checks, no presentation of identification. Does he need to know this? Maybe. She told me the story on the occasion of inviting me to speak at the college that employs her. I must have disappointed her, as she has, more or less, never responded to an email of mine from that day on. Perhaps like my grandmother's, my diction was not exactly what was hoped for.

We are at a birthday party when my brother tells me his story and I don't tell him mine, and he has probably paraphrased and I am probably paraphrasing here, as I retell it. The party was for my nephew's daughter, turning sixteen, getting ready to take her road test. She is active in the Longhouse, more active than I'll ever be, currently developing a school project on the Industrial School at Carlisle that is now removed from her by five generations, a hint and suggestion instead of on display daily in heartbreak and guarded distance. She is collaging photos and integrating texts, and I have hope because there is little I can tell her that she doesn't already know, and she knows things I never will. Like many of us, she is particularly attracted to two kinds of photographs, the Before and the After. Maybe someday, when I tell her a story where the facts are not exactly right, where I have been a more articulate person than I am, a better-mannered person, she will not interrupt, will listen carefully, anyway, to hear what might have been killed, what might have survived.

Jaboozie Brings My Aunt Home, Unexpectedly

Jaboozie asks what I was doing
in Texas, wondering if I were like my aunt
who claimed her life was a country and western
song, that she left "all of her exes in Texas,"
though my aunt had no exes there, that I knew of,
her only boyfriend following her husband's death,
a wild French Canadian I can barely remember,
beyond the photo of him with a shotgun and a moose's head
that kept her end table company, even years after
he no longer did the same favor for her.

Jaboozie delivers a lament like no one
I know, choosing exactly the sort of memory
to embrace loss, reminding me how even in her seventies,
my mother's sister made the kids laugh, teaching them
how to do the Twist, and man, she could Twist the night away
maybe having learned to do it with her crazy French Canadian
whose ears stuck out like open car doors—my aunt was
a serious twister in her day and even beyond.

Jaboozie only has half the story, as is often
the case, when you marry into a family, not knowing,
for example, how my aunt politely explained
to a disabled man from down the road that it was
not a good thing to look in the bedroom windows
of widowed women, then as he left her Thermopane
for the last time, how she grabbed
the neighborhood tomcat by the tail, the one
that always tried to break into her
house whenever she opened the door

and flung it yards away, instructing it
to "never come back, fucker," laughing
to herself, despite her better judgment,
as the man jumped
a little, reaching the road.

Jaboozie had never seen
the photograph we lost in the fire of my aunt,
taken sometime in the '50s, wearing a long,
tight-fitting dress patterned in black and white
horizontal stripes, an outfit we called
her "Hamburglar dress," after that McDonald's
commercial character, because we refused to see
her that far back in the past, a beautiful reservation
woman in a provocative outfit, ready
to twist at a moment's notice, should the right man
come along, knowing as we would
know into the future, that she would
love twice, maybe even three times, but that she would
be alone at the end.

Jaboozie receives no answer
from me, as her question merely opens doors for us
to remember the ways my aunt was
more exotic and alive than the Twist,
and certainly more dangerous than a country
and western song, and there, for that moment, we have
brought her back, each in our own way.

Hunger Test: Primer Revisited

The first book I learned to read/memorize
was called *Snuggles*. It was an instructional
picture book, full of repetition and basic
ideas, as such books often are. My siblings,
much older than I was, read it to me over
and over, until I knew which words went
with which pictures, eventually learning
which sequences and combinations of letters
and numbers spelled out the words and
sentences I'd already committed to reciting.

I find a copy years later, and send pictures
to my siblings, none needing much
to remind them of vivid details. My
brother just a few years older, surprises
me by listing, immediately, parts of
the main character's convoluted name.
Maybe it was his before mine, passed down.

None of us seem to recall it is basically
a "counting" book, where the character,
a gray kitten, learns to count from one
to seven, a useful skill for beginning readers.

Instead, we recall its strange art, real cats manipulated
in miniature settings and situations, dressed in old
fashioned outfits, the kinds of clothes we might see
old Indians wearing on their way to church, or taking
their place in the audience at the annual Christmas pageant.

We misremember the title, or maybe I am alone
in this forgetfulness. I have believed for all this time,

the book is actually called *Snuggles, the Greedy*
Kitten, which tells you the nature of this story.

It was published after the Great Depression
in America and is about a kitten who takes,
throughout the very short story, more than her
fair share. Her mother tends mostly to a younger
kitten and her father is distracted by his work.
Her grandmother is present but Snuggles pretends,
like grandchildren everywhere, not to hear her disapproval.

Snuggles, left to her own desires, seeks out more
food, and eventually pays the price for her greed,
is given medicine and sent to bed, promising to change.

Our old copy is long gone, and even if it had been absently
stored in some obscure corner of our Dog Street house,
it would have gone up in flames with the rest of our
belongings and history we hadn't found places for.

Though I eventually found it online at eBay, everyone's
dream repository, and revisited its details with clarity, we had
no need if we were just remembering the lessons we had
to internalize. It lives on, the name Snuggles evolving into
a family code word we used to remind ourselves, and each
other, that hunger and greed exist only shadows
apart from each other on the spectrum of need.

Making Promises

My sister calls me
the day I have set aside
to finish this set of poems
I have agreed to have
completed by a certain
date rushing fast at me,
and though she asks casually
what I am doing, I know she is
calling for an entirely different
reason I will have to wait to hear—
that she needs my help in convincing
our mother to see
a doctor, and though I don't
know why she thinks my voice will
make any difference, I put on
my coat and boots and wait
for her to summon me explicitly
because this is a silent promise
she has made me, that she will deliver
bad news as if it is a breeze building
up speed to hurricane force only eventually
so I will have time
to brace myself and lean
against the wind.

The Ethnographer Turns the Rorschach Cards on Himself

After fifty years away, the social scientist
who specialized in us returns. Back then, he
showed my grandmother inkblots and asked
about what she saw, and this time, he decides
to write about our community. Without
realizing it, he actually writes about his
time in our midst instead of our own.

He admits that the first time he arrived, seventeen
years before I was born, he even stayed briefly
at Little Umma's home. They broke bread
as he tried to understand who we were and
what mysteries we saw in those ambiguous,
controlled spills of ink on paper, one side
exactly mirroring the other, like wampum.

In his eventual book, he can find no true place
for my voice, because as an Onondaga in my
family, I am forever *from* Tuscarora, but also
eternally not *of* Tuscarora, as if my life lacking
symmetry did not truly exist, as if mine was
the voice of a ghost, since he could not find
a place to file it, in the real world of his ordering.

Because I am now more than an asterisk, inconvenient
footnote, he feels he must include some comment, tucked
beneath Ted C. Williams, the Tuscarora writer and artist
who showed me what was possible all those years ago.

But what the Ethnographer says reveals more
about him, than it does about me. I am his inkblot,
as he casually rearranges and changes details
of my life, claims fully clothed women in my
paintings are "naked," and sees a hero in my
fiction where there is none. He imagines he sees
Bruce Wayne on the page instead of the Joker
truly residing there, and like him fifty years ago,
I am now here to record my own impressions
for posterity and anyone from my community,
seven generations down the line, who might
wonder what things were like "back then."

"We Had Some Good Times Anyway"

This is what she whispers
to me, my mother, as we embrace,
hold one another just
before they close the casket
for the last time
at your funeral.
This is what she
could summon, build,
conjure, after having
been married
to you more
or less for over
fifty years.

Do you wonder after all
this time has passed
to what she might be
referring as she lets go
of those few tears
she generally keeps
locked within that smile?

I tend to think
they are not the times
you smashed cars she had
not yet paid for
or those when you would
disappear without warning
or at least not directly.

Instead they are the ways
we reinvented ourselves

in your absence, the ways
we became whole
without you, learning
to eat fast before someone
else proved Darwin only partially
right to a group of people
who would have never believed
him even if they had heard
of his survival theories. We knew
what Darwin could have never found
room for, humor and invention
keeping us from the endangered list.

In the twenty years between the day I moved
out of the Dog Street house you never lived in
anyway, and the day we settled you in with your
clan row in the upper mountain cemetery, I am not
sure I saw you more than ten times: at least once
in a bar; once in a hospital; once at a family picnic;
once at a funeral; and least believable, once at a party
I hosted. I am not sure if I should count the time
a young woman who wanted to get to know me
better befriended you with free drinks, hoping
for information you couldn't possibly have, and
I am not sure if I should count the days I spent
with family cleaning up every bit of chaos you
left behind in a two-room apartment
in a city where the rest of us never lived.

The Ethnographer Leaves Us a Gift

When he asks Little Umma, my grandmother,
and a large swath of her friends and enemies,
what they saw in those blotchy psychological
tests, he also had the foresight to record
them speaking to one another in Tuscarora.

Maybe what he saw in the inkblot shaped
like Tuscarora Nation, was the Carlisle
legacy slowly playing out just as planned.
If those who returned spoke strictly English
to their children, it would only be a matter of
decades before our language disappeared
entirely, and we'd be left with no alternative
but to think in English, an inexact version
of our lives, like a TV channel stuck between
signals from two different stations. Our eyes
and ears would eventually choose the stronger
one as the weaker transmissions faded into snow.

It is 1948, before magnetic tape becomes
the portable preserver of sight and sound. In this
way, we are in luck, as tape demagnetizes
and vanishes left to itself. The Ethnographer
has instead hooked up his wire recorder
and generously documented "Conversational
Tuscarora" in all its nuance and unexpected
angles, abrupt stops, and narrow alleys.

He files all of these wire recordings in the archives
of the American Philosophical Association,

in Philadelphia, the city where Willard Gansworth
married Nellie May Patterson, so near Carlisle,
before they decided it was time for them to Get Back
to the reservation to see what they could salvage.

These recordings would wait patiently
for us to awaken, and discover them,
reconstructing our memories, one syllable,
one pause, one considered thought at a time.

Maybe what he sees is my niece, back from
her own far-reaching journeys, settling in
at Onondaga. She begins slowly, first making
Elders meals they remember from their own
younger years, meals she reconstructs out
of her own memories of eating in our house,
at my mother's table, our improvised recipes
made from End of the Month ingredients. She
eventually runs a community farm, growing
heritage seeds, saving our flavor and sustenance
for future generations, teaching others to join her.

Maybe what he sees is my nephew, marrying
traditionally, and despite having too many
nicknames to keep track of, he is the first
of us to go through Naming Ceremony
at Midwinters, doing it right. Maybe he sees
that nephew make the feast of enough Indian
Cornbread for every person attending his wedding,
repeating the ritual, showing he knows how
to provide for the family that will keep
growing as he and his new wife step into
the role of the next generation of parents.

Maybe what he sees is that nephew's son, learning himself how to plant traditionally, as a boy, long before he joins his auntie in her heritage garden, while he completes his own college education, balancing both of our worlds, the way each of us continues to do, one step and one breath at a time.

Or maybe it's that nephew's daughter, now grown, having finished college, and immersing herself in a language restoration program, accessing a thumb drive, and downloading the voice of her great-great-grandmother, telling the Ethnographer everything she thinks her family may need to hear generations distant from her own, not yet developed, not yet dreamed into this world, by connections between two people still insisting on perpetuating our way of life in every possible act that they can.

I Gain a Ribbon Shirt in Bloodlines

In a community this small, this tight,
if you are an outsider, you will be reminded.
We learn this early and are reminded often.
Some reminders are easier to receive than others.

When my nephew gets married, his bride
is Tuscarora, the younger sister of friends
I went to Catholic Charities camp with
when we were kids, spending our first
nights away from the Rez together,
huddled in the midst of city poor kids,
the only Indians for miles and miles around.

In a community that small, that tight,
if you are an outsider, you will be reminded.
We learn this early and are reminded often.
Some reminders are tougher to receive than others.

Our memories of camp are mostly shadows,
fear, and becoming aware of what it meant
to make a community, even if it only
consisted of three boys from one tiny Rez.

All these years later, when my nephew
and his fiancée plan their wedding, he tans
the hide for his leggings and she beads
her outfit, preparing themselves for their
commitment to each other, to their future.
They are getting married at her brother's
place, across the road from the house

where they were raised. I assume he
and I will joke about our dark campground
nights impossibly away from home.

They ask me if I will design their wedding
invitations, including both of their clans. As he
is an Eel, like me, and she is a Turtle, I think
it will be easy, to have them following the same
path in a body of water, beneath the moon.
But I rarely draw animals, and I have to do
it over and over again until I get it right
enough to show anyone else, right enough
to represent them and their futures together.

When I give the drawing to them, they tell me
her sister will sew me a ribbon shirt to wear,
if I pick out my materials. At the fabric store,
I select ribbons I like, black, purple, lilac,
with matching silk thread, to go on a calico
of grapes, with vines and leaves on black.

She asks how long I want the ribbons to stream
and I say the length of the shirt, trying to picture
other traditional ribbon shirts in my mind, realizing
that I have retained only the haziest of details. She
delivers and I wear it, realizing we are both a part
of the ritual, exchanging our talents as part of
building the bridge between two families.

During the reception, I notice that every other
ribbon shirt around me has broader ribbons,
with short streamers. Mine would have been

much harder to sew, and as the sun sets around
us, she confirms, laughing, that she cursed me out
numerous times, having to rip ribbons out and start
again because she'd wandered off being distracted
even only for a second, thinking about something else.

We've known each other her entire life and our jokes
are not polite. She says she gained some new calluses
on her fingertips working on my overly busy shirt,
so if I spot some blood anywhere, it's my own fault
for my bold choices. I ask why she didn't just tell
me to pick out something different, less challenging.

She says that is not the way this works. I did my
part, and by these rights, she had to do hers.

In a community this small, this tight, there are
always compromises, you will be reminded.
We learn this early and are reminded often.
Some reminders are harder to receive than others.

When we are born outsiders, we sometimes
find bridges we can make with our own stories
embracing the ways they are connected, instead
of pointing out the gaps between the two sides.

Indian Picnic Cornbred

1.

So it's that Friday and Saturday in July, what we call the Weekend of the National Picnic at home, or what a lot of people call Indian Picnic, somehow forgetting all of our picnics are Indian Picnics. To this one, though, we don't bring dishes-to-pass. National Picnic is an open-to-the-public event, where we invite white people to join us, and the food passing from one hand to another is from vendors, requiring dollar bills to pass in exchange, the way it works outside the reservation. And the money, yes, the money, goes into that fund called "The Nation," and though I have never known the specific beneficiaries of that fund, I still buy overpriced water and frybread and Cornsoup because the taste of home is worth it and where else will I find it?

2.

There are fewer vendors this year, and the woodsmoke smell usually permeating the grove is absent along with the people who would light that fire and set the kettle on top and sit around it on folding chairs, waiting for the water to heat, and despite what you've heard, a watched pot does eventually boil, particularly when you focus your mind on the story at hand in the setting sun, and not on the water. And eventually, steam and water dance on the surface. These missing people are from the family who generally make Cornbread (no, not that yellow kind you get with barbecue—this is made from Indian corn, dried, lyed, and ground, mixed with kidney beans, without flour, shaped with water into large oval bricks, and thrown into a vat of boiling water until the loaves rise to the surface) so I know I won't be getting Cornbread this year, and already people can tell the difference. Next year, they might call this "The Year There Wasn't Any Cornbread" or "The Year They Stopped Bringing Cornbread." For my sake, I hope it is just the one year and not a permanent new condition, because I have no idea how to make it.

285

3.

My nephew knows how and his father-in-law grows Indian corn, but usually, my nephew makes Soup rather than Bread from the dried ears of Indian corn, and the preparation is so difficult, it is not the kind of thing you can ask someone to bring to a regular Indian picnic. They might ask, "What can I bring?" and you say back, "Whatever you want," and hope for the best. Sometimes it is Indian Tacos, and sometimes it is Cornsoup, and almost never is it these loaves of pressed corn that have been boiled in ashes and dried and manipulated to resemble bread. These loaves, my nephew had to make hundreds of them the day before he was married, all those years ago, because after the wedding ceremony, during the reception, tradition required him to walk around and offer pieces to every guest, from his arm to theirs, his hand to theirs, cut from loaves he carried in a basket, to show he would be a good provider for his future family and after the hours and hours of that ritual, how could anyone blame him for not making Cornbread very often?

4.

But this family, the ones who are not here this year, their usual spot near the parking field and a couple yards from the cookhouse, this is one of the things they do and are known to do. This is their gig. They know which rocks to gather for their circle, which wood to dry for kindling, for stoking, for maintaining. They know the right weight and shape to form the oval loaves, and this is no small thing. My nephew tells me that spring he is trading information with Fillipe, a half-assed cousin-in-law of ours who is teaching him the traditional songs. In return for the songs, and the voice and the place to sing them, he is showing Fillipe the half-assed cousin-in-law how to make Cornbread. I ask him why he is giving up his secrets. He says self-defense. He says: "I ate some of that Cornbread he's selling now, trying to pay his past-due bills before his electric gets cut off, and it's so nasty that there isn't a non-brain-damaged person out here who will buy it. If I don't show him how to make the Cornbread right, he's gonna starve to death, and then who will I go to for my songs? Supply and demand."

5.

And that year's National Picnic Friday, when I stop at the burnt-out foundation and new-growth trees that had been the house I grew up in, where I make sure to visit at least once a year, to remember my home, I hear someone call from an open window next door and I cross the growth between their house and my memory. One of my cousins is in the window. Her father is from across the customs border and his name is Joe, and because this is the reservation we give him the last name "Canada" and sing his name like the National Anthem of that country minutes north of us. He's okay with it because he knows we only make those distinctions when we are forced to, declaring "North American Native" when asked our citizenship at the customs office. His daughter in the window is a woman who grew up here and in Hamilton, and who knows the loss of home fires herself, having caused theirs at the age of four, combining matches and curiosity in the family's hall closet. She asks if I have gotten the new Tragically Hip CD.

6.

I tell her "of course," and she demands we listen to it right then and there, so I drive the few yards between our places, pop my trunk, and we sit on the front porch my uncle the carpenter made in his spare time. The Canadian side of her DNA wakes up, and since we don't consider it another country, the Canadian side of my DNA wakes up as well, as we listen to Gordon Downie singing of poets and hockey and ice storms and hockey and Toronto and hockey and penguins and hockey and fireworks and the power of phantoms, or fleeting, phantom power, and in return, she walks in the house and returns, offering me slices of Cornbread, buttered and salted, on a paper towel. I taste it and everything is as it should be despite the fact that my home has been gone for years and in another couple, the foundation will be lost to trees striving for light, but because the house was lost to a fire caused by an accident involving her father, the only ashes we discuss are those used in one step of making the Cornbread.

7.

She says she bought it at the Picnic from Fillipe, and I understand that my nephew's new singing voice was not traded to him in vain, as Fillipe has found the way to our memory and information passed on for generations. I understand that recipes and songs are not that far removed from one another and as we listen to the last Hip song the second time through, a piece about the endurance of Emperor Penguins and the things they do to help their families survive, huddling together and turning themselves against the wind, I finally see she has set down beside her a half a loaf of Cornbread, neatly wrapped in tinfoil, which she hands to me as I climb in my car to head for the city. "For home," she says, "for home, and when you get there and need a taste of here."

Ash and Smoke

1.

Your cigarette-end-filled glass
trays with soot, gray like steel
wool, endless. We'd empty
them only when they could bear
no more without spilling.
If we gather, flake by flake, these
remains, could we re-form
you, like those bodies in Pompeii,
or would you burst, like dandelion
seed, fly on the breeze, and settle
across the reservation, transplanting
yourself in unexpected places, taking
root, between driveway stones, foundations,
lawns of Indian men trying on suburbia
while their bodies hold out? Even overcast,
on those days the swamp has burned
or someone has lighted the dike with gasoline
again to kill last year's weeds,
and the sky washes out
like pulpy newspaper pictures,
could you thrive in those
most inhospitable places?

2.

You knew the power
of ash, for though your mother
so rejected our lives
and histories, she threatened
physical violence to the reservation

schoolteacher who tried to teach
you the art of water drums and beads
as the twentieth century began,
she still taught you
the steps, one by one,
of making soup from the braids
of dried corn hanging
in the tractor shed,
and while the first step
requires the unbraiding
of ears, allowing them to drop
to the dirt floor, the second
involves a look to the sky
searching for woodsmoke.

3.

When you want to lye
some corn for soup, you beg
around the reservation at homes
with cords lining backyards
for the months
we only glimpse the sun
if they can spare
a few bucketsful.
After you pour ashes
over corn in boiling water,
split it, swell it, rinse
and rinse and rinse and rinse,
dry, season, resubmerge in clean
stock with beans and pig hocks,
we will be expected to return
the favor, divide

our soup with the people
who gave us piles of gray flakes
from their fireplaces, as if
they were saving it
for something special.

4.

Hardwood is best,
you say, sifting through
swollen-knuckled fingers
this powder, warning
us to stand back
and not breathe
in this cloud, tapping
your precious enameled pot,
saying bare metal would dissolve
but the dried corn finds
new life for us in the ash.

5.

Kerosene burns without ash,
smoke alone rising, blackening
our chimney, roof, lungs
and later, when the kerosene
heater goes the way
of full-bloods, natural gas
leaves nothing in the sky
above our house, except vapor
trails in the winter nights.
Yet, when that car flies
into our dining room wall,
igniting propane tanks,

personal-sized bombs,
we discover all the hardwood
we would need
for a lifetime of soup,
our home raining these riches
down on us, smudges of trees
killed and dried over
a century before, while
firemen soaked the place
from water-truck hoses
not to save it, but to stop
it from traveling to woods
and nearby houses, all
potential ash, living and dead,
and that day we lost one half
of our history to fire
one quarter to water
one quarter to ash.

6.

When you start over,
you refuse to go back,
won't even ride by
in a car, the spot
where new hardwood,
smoke and flames years clear,
pushes itself through
ash and foundation stones,
and you take what new things
we've been able to re-create,
into a small bedroom
of another son's trailer

where you put out Kool 100s
even if you have just
sparked it that moment
whenever you recognize
the sound of my footsteps
and always, as I enter
the room where the walls
and ceilings slowly turn
the rich brown of nicotine,
you brush ashes
from your blouse,
from your slacks,
from your fingers,
where the smallest flecks
climb inside those prints
scarred from years
of carrying in kerosene cans
and years of sticking them
into lying corn, stripping
germ and hull, and though
you pretended you were
impervious, we both know
better,
and leave trails across your clothes
and whatever else you might touch,
a signature, of sorts.

7.

Did I rise to the insignificant
height of five foot, six inches
because I was a nicotine baby,
or because I learned early

embracing your habit
at the age of thirteen,
and quitting at nineteen,
too late for bones
to recover, or were we meant
to be small, for as I hug you,
the last time we speak,
your eighty-first
birthday, I notice how small
you have become, these thirty-nine
and a half years after giving birth
to me, your seventh and last,
you have shrugged off that life,
transformed into a bird, a cat,
a dandelion, ready to seed,
and a moment later, you disappear
into your bedroom, away from
laughing children, and grandchildren
and great-grandchildren, where air is
made up of less oxygen than usual,
those of us who smoke surrounding
you in blue swirls
of secondhand carcinogens,
their clothes dotted
with holes the right size
to capture a nighttime star
or follow an eclipse across
a sheet of paper—even shaded
we cannot look directly in
to the face of Elder Brother,
who will burn our corneas clean—
no smoke or ash, just cloudy

scar tissue—without a second glance.
We confirm in the haze I will be
back in a day, two at the most
so you can teach me how
to make frybread, though you warn
me, white people will not like it.
You want to add a little sugar,
make it more to their taste
and I say I want it just the way
you always make it, and a grandchild
says you had better tip in some ashes
from the cigarette between your lips
when you knead the dough.

8.

Those last few
days after the stroke,
a week and a half
after the neurologist
said you would never come
back, and we should be thankful
that you would not awaken,
a week and a half after
we have brought you home,
a hospital bed replacing
your smoking chair
in the living room,
we care for you, the best
we can, and though you do not
awaken, as predicted, we get you
socks to keep your feet
warm, and their whiteness looks

strange as you were
a lifelong knee-highs lady
and because my niece puts them on
you, the newly pronounced soul reflexes
offer a map of your journey
away from us, administered
by the hands of a smoker,
leaving small traces of gray
marks, one tiny slash for each hope.

9.

And after the EMT wraps you
in a cocoon, slowly drawing
the zipper closed, as he lifts
the gurney, shutting the door
and driving you off the reservation
another niece reveals a lighter,
a shell, tobacco, an eagle feather,
and ignites our loss, on this cold
November night, the Celestial road
clear and distinct above us. She fans
the tobacco smoke, and what rises
to circle the moon, head home
to the Skyworld,
is our loss,
your spirit,

some smoke,

a little ash.

Howdy Prepares for the Future

By the time the twentieth century
became the twenty-first, he understood
the Ethnographer was right, and he believed
no recordings of old friends were going
to be enough to save our language
living within our ears and hearts.

Howdy, beyond his eightieth year, kept
talking and talking, with young and old
alike, making guest appearances in classes,
answering questions as one by one, everyone
else he could converse with in Tuscarora
went back to the Skyworld, leaving him
here to chat with us in every clumsy
failing and misstep we took along the way.

He spent days developing worksheets for
us, organized by whatever was on his mind
at the moment, whatever he felt was important
when he sat down: grooming, hygiene, eating,
socializing, knowing your relatives, knowing
your animals and—because he had been around
in the lean years—how to identify and care
for the sick without becoming ill, yourself.
It must have worked because he stuck around
until he was 96, in the Good Mind to the very end.

The last few years, he met regularly, almost
every day, with a small group of attentive
listeners, discreetly working against time

to fill their ears, maybe carrying on with
that outside tradition of recording, preserving
for the time when no new sounds would be forthcoming.

My nephew is at the forefront, spending days
and days learning, improving, learning by
improving. He is a talented musician and is
accustomed to transposing one set of sounds
for another, one language for another. Before
Howdy leaves, my nephew can step forward
at a formal gathering, deliver our Thanksgiving
Address smoothly, without hesitation, allowing
us to make our way forward, with the dignity
and grace we deserve, into our endless future.

I listen to him speak with joy and regret I was
not born a little earlier, a little later, wishing
I had more discipline and freer time when we found
our way back home, on our way back home.

Instead, with Howdy's silence stretching
out before us, I look at the photocopied
worksheets he left behind in my possession,
the information he felt we needed most, most
urgently, and I can't help but feel like I'm
Lost in Time, Lost in Space, Lost in Translation.

Lost (in Translation)

The old man says	Haw Oo-nunh-hah-ah Raw-nee-haw Weh-rhah-Ke-eh-rheh
"I am listening	Whaw-kaw-teh-naw'
to the rain."	neh-wheh'-dooj
He is	Trah-ya-nueh teh Hek-yeh
this one of	Keh'n nuh Ehh-chee Oo-nuh-skee-uh
one little	Ehh-chee uh
two little	Nak-dee uh
three little	Aww-sehh uh
you know,	Sha-nah-reeth
Indians	Ihk-wheh-hih-wheh
four little	Hit-duhk uh
five little	Weesk uh
five little	Weesk uh
yes,	Naw-hwess
that's it	Ha nuh hek-yeh T'wa'hn
five little	Weesk uh
Indians who speak	Ihk-wheh-hih-wheh Koh-na Ah-kah Weh Ree-uhk
the Tuscarora language.	Ska-rhu-rheh
Come, look,	Gotchee! Sah-uh,
and listen	dees-neh Thawd' haeh-naw' naehd
to what he gave me.	Daw-wheah-deh Whah-raw-Kweh
He says:	Weh-rhah-Ke-eh-rheh
I will braid your hair	Eh-kaw-daw-thah-de Thaw-kyeah'-whaw-weh
	Eh Sneh-wheh-de
He says:	Weh-rhah-Ke-eh-rheh

We are going to church	Eh-nwaw-rooj-raeh-deh
He says:	Weh-rhah-Ke-eh-rheh
We will sing in church	Eh-nwaw-rhee-whawk Yeah'-rooj-raeh-kwaw
He says:	Weh-rhah-Ke-eh-rheh
I am sick	Whawk-naeh-whawks
He says:	Weh-rhah-Ke-eh-rheh
I have a cold	Whah-kawd-hoo-sah-ryeah-thaeh
He says:	Weh-rhah-Ke-eh-rheh
I will blow my nose	Eh-keh-dee-jeh'-seh
He says:	Weh-rhah-Ke-eh-rheh
I have a fever	Whaw-kaw-nar-whawks
He says:	Weh-rhah-Ke-eh-rheh
I have diarrhea	Nah-whaw-kweh-kooth
He says:	Weh-rhah-Ke-eh-rheh
Does he have diarrhea?	Nah-raw-wheh'-kooth-heh?
He says:	Weh-rhah-Ke-eh-rheh
Does she have diarrhea?	Naw-weh'-kooth-heh?
He says:	Weh-rhah-Ke-eh-rheh
You caught it	Whah-shah-neh
He says:	Weh-rhah-Ke-eh-rheh
You gave me the sickness	Whaws-koo-doo-raw-weh
He says:	Weh-rhah-Ke-eh-rheh
You spread the sickness	Whaws-koo-doo-rah-dyoo
He says:	Weh-rhah-Ke-eh-rheh
What's the matter with you?	Daw-wheh-deh hek-yeh-dee-thaeth?
He says:	Weh-rhah-Ke-eh-rheh
Do you care?	Sree-whaws-heh?
He says:	Weh-rhah-Ke-eh-rheh
Who do you care for?	Kaw-neh-shah-naes-neh?
He says:	Weh-rhah-Ke-eh-rheh
Do you care for me?	Sknaes-neh-heh?
He says:	Weh-rhah-Ke-eh-rheh

I care for you.	Kah-neas-neh
He says:	Weh-rhah-Ke-eh-rheh
You care for me.	Skneas-neh
He says:	Weh-rhah-Ke-eh-rheh
He cares for me.	Rawk-neas-neh
He says:	Weh-rhah-Ke-eh-rheh
She cares for me.	Yaek-naes-neh
He says:	Weh-rhah-Ke-eh-rheh
Nothing more	Ees-ehd Tsah wunh teh
so this is all we have.	Keh'n nuh hek-yeh T'wa'hn
He is fantasizing	Rawd-keh Neh-dee
that I have heard	Ha nuh Wah-hek Heh-sheh
all he has said	T'wa'hn Weh-rhah-Ke-eh-rheh
as I walk away	Whot-Go(t) Haw-Hawk
saying "What did you say?"	Whaw-khee-rhae Daw-wheh-deh Whah-see-rhae?
"I did not understand."	Deh-Eh'K-dee-keh Rah-yeah-nah
What he saw	Hoh heh'n Daw-Wheh-Deh
was me walking on	ee-ee Ah ree-uh ra kwunk
the Bad Road	haw Wah-hah HawK-seh
with the white people.	dees-neh Crhee-rhoo-rhia-kyeah.
Quietly	nhawsd
without bitterness	Gwah-ess You-Chee-Whah-Kenh Oo-nuh-skee-uh
He says:	Weh-rhah-Ke-eh-rheh
"Did you hear?"	Weh-Thaw-heh-sheh-Heh?
"Do you hear the rain?"	"Whaw-rhaw-kaw-teh-naw' neh wheh-dooj heh?"

And on This Day, We Commence

In cap and gown and hood
that distinguishes me
from my colleagues, asserting
I am only a Master, not a Doctor,
I stand on the auditorium steps, ready
to brace myself for the speech
of this is not the end, this is a new
beginning, a new chapter, a new book,
a new life, a new love, a new day
that sounds very much like days before
it, but I go, every year, not
because it is my job, but because I want
to see these young people
I have known in some cases
for four years, have watched
as they grew outward
and inward, reflective
and expectant, as they leave
and move into adulthood,
buying groceries, insurance,
electricity, worrying
as month and paycheck collide,

when my sister-in-law
calls my cell phone, and I reach
into the shirt pockets
hidden in all this velvet
and satin. She tells me
about a young man from home,
an in-law once removed, the child

of my nephew's brother-in-law, a boy I had
written a poem about, a few
short years ago, after watching him
dance a traditional, across a gymnasium
floor, sneaker becoming moccasin, moving
with the ease of someone who learned
these steps as a baby. This boy
has died sometime before the sun
rose, beginning the celebration of
his twenty-fifth birthday, just
after midnight, finding one
of those reservation trees
that draw so many of our young
like earthbound beacons, daring
us to meet at dangerous speeds
and survive. In the twenty-first
century, is this the vision
quest, the challenge, the way
we prove ourselves at home? Was I
just lucky enough that I had no car,
no license, when I was accepted
at my open admissions college?

That night, after hanging
my hood for another year,
at the wake, I see he will be
buried with his lacrosse stick,
wood carved from a tree, caressed
and bent to the will of man, and I run
into old friends, men my age,
and we lean on one another,
in the dark, only firelight

giving us glimpses of each other,
surrounded, as we are, by those same
trees. One of us sundances every year
and no, it isn't me—that hook has not
pierced my chest, dragged me along. Though
they know other things tie me in different
moves, different circles, we all know
we have been that boy, chasing trees
at eighty miles an hour and coming out
on the other side. We remember
laughing hysterically, piling out
to look at our tread burns,
the marks we tried to make
back then, when our ceremonies,
our offerings, were less
complicated, more dangerous.

We remember those among
our friends who didn't reach
this stage, before the smile
creases in our faces grew
into permanent worry lines.

This fire at the wake
will go on all night, tended
by his lacrosse teammates,
other young men offering harnessed wood
and tobacco to send ash and smoke
into the night, the Celestial path home,
and we know that in the late
or early hours, we will hear
tires squeal, and we will wait

for the sound that may
or may not come, the sound
of another generation challenging
the trees of home, the laws
of gravity and motion, as they begin
to cross the stage, waiting
for their names to be called.

Dog Street, July 3, 2009

An hour short of America
kicking off its independence
celebration for the two hundred
and thirty-third time, I linger
near the reservation center
stop sign, my homeplace cross, a strip
of pavement dividing the reservation
northern and southern halves,
where street signs are written
in English, in white and green
reflector paint and above them,
in purple and white, phonetic
Tuscarora place names. Green claims
the legal Mount Hope, and I want the purple
to say Dog Street. I look to the school
where I had learned to write and speak
English and Tuscarora for six years,
still embarrassed I stole a glance
at my cousin's first-grade paper, cheating
to spell our last name right.

I've been out doing Rez laps in my pistol-grip
six-speed "Hemi Orange" Challenger, new, but
retro-styled, five years of big payments ahead.

My left and right shoulders spike
electrical flame to my brain
when I shift gears, small fires
down the two-way streets between
arms and brain, part of the deluxe package

for this forty-four-year-old body,
a lot of mileage but no broken
bones so far. My neighbor,
a nurse who kindly offers
medical advice (mostly
when I ask) says gravity
has pinched cervical nerves
as they wander the guide
holes flanking the central vertebral
foramen where the spinal cord rests,
protected by bone, cartilage, and muscle.

I nod, hearing a slight skull base grinding,
just below the inion, between the two specialized
vertebrae before the spine proper begins,
remembering the skull and globe
of the brainpan rests on the atlas,
and just below it, the axis allowing for maximum
cranial rotation, or it did before a couple months ago,
when the grinding began. From sliding those dry bones
together to see how they function in college anatomy
classes, I can grasp the realities of these sounds
playing new songs at my bump of knowledge.

I avoided football injuries and the car
crashes most of my friends experienced
in our high school years, because I was
uncoordinated and car-less, and while
it's true, I drive home to wind the car's
tachometer out to redline on our unpatrolled
roads now, being a better and more responsible
driver than the average seventeen-year-old, I am still

fairly careful, or maybe just a lucky person, and yet, here
I sit, wondering if my arms will soon be too weak
to work the transmission of the car I can finally afford.

But when headlights suddenly appear
in my rearview mirror, and the horn honks,
I pound the gas, blast through the intersection
and shift for performance, head toward
the ghost of my old home, and the unmoving
reservoir slouching where Dog Street ends,
and as the speedometer flies to eighty, those lights
stay on my ass and knowing we're about to hit
the S-curves, I let them get the edge and pass.

Illuminated in my low beams, two young people
huddle on a four-wheel All-Terrain Vehicle, their
long hair, unhelmeted, whipping in the wind tunnel
they create, unable or unwilling to imagine the risks
they are taking. I didn't think ATVs could make it up
to speeds like that, but those two seem like they've been
doing this forever, and will keep on at that pace
at least until one of them flies off to a different future.

I keep going straight, but after they pass me, they
cut a sharp right, forcing me to brake, and they barely
make the turn onto Green Road, a sparsely populated
strip that exists only on the Rez. It takes you from one Rez
road to another, a closed circuit where I assume there
is a party starting this Fourth of July weekend. I slow,
but do not turn my head to witness the final
destination of those taillights, where they come
to rest, and I keep going straight. When I arrive

at the end of Dog Street, the reservoir fills
my vision for four stories, blocking my view
of the Skyworld above, the place we all return to.
Stretching beyond both ends of my peripherals, I see
the street sign dead ahead.

There is no English, no Tuscarora,
no words, just a straight horizontal line
with an arrow head at each end,
giving you only two options: leave
north or leave south. This intersection
I know best. It is the head of Dog Street,
the place it inevitably ends and I don't
even need to be able to crane my neck
to point myself one way or the other,
the route I committed to memory twenty-five
years before, when I was too comfortable
with the siren call, loving life without the luxury
of a helmet, inviting premature damage
to axis and atlas, and the shattering
of knowledge's bump at the same time.

Lost and Found on Dog Street

(for Lynda Barry)

1.

There is no Dog Street Lost and Found, but because
we are beings of reinvention, some people claim
there is, searching in the Community Building clothing
donation room as needs change with seasons. They pick
up an item they know someone else has delivered, Gently
Used, and say loudly, so others can hear, "Oh, I can't believe
I found this! So careless! I must have set it down and walked
away. Such good luck someone picked it up and brought it here."

On those racks and in those bins, I have left
a future for someone to find, returning the favor
a hundred others have done for me. I can afford new
clothes right now, but almost everything I wear first
belonged to someone else, first was lived in, by a stranger.
White people, embarrassed to say they are willingly
wearing clothes someone else has sweated in, call
this "Vintage," as if old Levi's grow like grapes,
as if you could lift these faded jeans and note
their bouquet, their body, and all the other
fancy wine terms no one on the Rez would note.

Sometimes, I can guess the shape of my jeans'
former owner, by all the ways they are broken
in, the contours of gravity and time on someone
else's body haunt these pants before I inhabit
them and change their shape, conform them to me.

2.

Every Friday in college, I try to catch up with all
the white people I spend days around, almost invisible
among them, but not quite, an ethnographer. But they
know something is off in me, even if they can't quite pin
it, or me, down. There is no Tutoring Center on campus
for this DNA-deep misunderstanding of "American Life
as a Second Language." My most reliable Rez to America
Translation Dictionary is a local arts paper, what they call
an Alternative Weekly. It appears every Thursday, stacked
in the noisy punk bars and college cafeterias where I do my
fieldwork, and in every store where you can find music
no one else has heard of, and other stores stacked with rows
of cheap wine in containers like milk cartons, but none
featuring the smiling fleeting faces of children gone missing.

Perched among concert listings, music and movie reviews,
are ads ads ads written by grieving people who've lost so many
handholds in their lives that they are willing to lay down good
money on the chance that some unknown and unknowable
other local, flipping through this weekly paper, will take pity,
have compassion, and be honest enough to return what they
have so carelessly lost, tracing the maps to their own lives.

3.

Lost: my first concert T-shirt
        (Captain & Tennille, and if you must know, yes, I made it)
Lost: purple and white cable sweater my grandmother knitted
        (before she forgot how to keep track of counting rows)
Lost: locket heart necklace where I hold my long-secret first love
        (it's the only photo I have, you can keep the charm. It's sterling)

Lost: black leather jacket, size 40, snaps and zippers
   (I know you stole it when I was drunk-peeing at the Continental,
   it was my dead brother's. Please, no questions asked)
Lost: ring my father gave me, for when I find the one
   (costume, family history, please do not pawn REWARD)
Lost: gerbil (Richard), snake (Adam), rat (Ben, I know, *how original*)
   (realistically, Richard and Ben might be inside Adam, but I'd like
   to know)
Lost: cat, patchy gray and cream, crossed eyes, part Siamese, answers to Blue
   (okay, flicks her ears if you say her name, but really, she knows)
Lost: heart, over and over and over and over
   (yes, I am careless this way and maybe
   deserve to lose every atrium and ventricle)

4.

The ads are 80 percent Lost and 20 percent Found, and
even my limited math skills allow me to see
how easy it is for finders to claim those objects
that weren't theirs but that fell into their laps,
   (especially if no one is looking
   and maybe even if someone is).

Desire sometimes throws Common Sense
into a long-term storage box against its will.

Found: your wallet, no cash, no cards
   (except for the library ha ha)
   (maybe you want this Prom Picture,
   and the brittle condom in the tattered sleeve)
Found: cat, patchy gray and cream, crossed eyes, part Siamese
   (sorry, I'm keeping it. You shouldn't be so careless)

5.

I don't know why I read them. Anything I've lost
is never coming back and I already know that.

Lost: the first painting I ever made, a mural across my bedroom wall.
Lost: the people I never knew how to thank when I was young.
Lost: the people I never knew how to love when I was young.
Lost: my uncle's songs, every one of them bound by his unmistakable yodel.
Lost: fluency in Tuscarora, thinking and speaking, imagining, of course.

6.

Yet, lurking among the ocean waves of mourning and denial
rendered in unstable newspaper ink that leaves your fingers dirty,
I find signals you send out, heartache and keys to survival
encrypted as comics of poor kids finding their own
way, through public pools and melting Popsicles and houses
falling apart like a slow Pompeii, walls flaking into ash.

How can a twilight Kickball Game be a life preserver?
The right song at the right moment cocoons me like amber.

We don't know each other, but discovering your work
feels like attending the most epic Rez family reunion
you ever remember, the kind you'd tell grandchildren
about, if you were reckless enough to send another
generation out into the world that tries to eat us.

7.

For many years, I don't have the equipment,
the voice, the venue to send signals back to you
across the continent. But eventually, our constant

Tests for Echo spanning unimaginable vastness
from our tiny, misshapen places, cross each other.

Our images find the homes we imagine when we lift
our pens and brushes for the first time, pinning
down voices people have tried, with great effort,
to erase from the air or deny us our whole lives.

8.

How does your ever-changing urban neighborhood
in Sixties Seattle sound so so much like the semi-
permanent, semi-permeable membrane my frozen
feet and stiffened, clumsy hands know as Dog Street,
the heart and aorta and spinal cord of my home?

How does Dog Street, in turn (with its wall-
to-wall stories of my endless relatives, so dense
it might as well house a Dog Street DNA dog tag),
find you, in songs I send out, all these years
after I first find your signals? The odds seem
as improbable as both of us Learning to Speak
despite all the odds actively working against us.

9.

When I take you there, I wonder if Dog Street
can possibly live up to your imagined version
because when I write about it, I see every incarnation
I know, 54 years overlaid like encyclopedia anatomy
transparencies, like the ghosts in every lame scary
movie you or I have ever seen, there and not there.

Movies never capture what it truly means to be haunted.

As I drive you to the heart, we stop at vacant,
wild places that leave almost no traces I ever lived
there, only the vague impressions I can describe
and try to raise the dead by the force of my voice.

10.

Lost: my family home, to fire in 1994
        (the same year I move into my last home)
Lost: much of its driveway, now leading nowhere
        (all our crushed stone sunk in mud, new grass covering)
Lost: the trees I climbed to reach the school roof
        (cut because we climbed them to reach the school roof)
Lost: the corner store where we walked for Popsicles and chips
        (that we always understood were luxuries)
Lost: my grandparents and parents and all aunts and uncles
        (how did I become an "Elder" in my forties?)

Found: bottle trees whistling on Green Road, framing potholes and cinders
        (and every story left untold, what happens on Green Road stays)
        (well, not always. Everyone loves a little Eee-ogg, don't they?)
Found: the graveyard has blossomed with solar-powered LEDs
        (and if we were here at night, they would be color-coordinated
        ghosts)
        (but we won't be here at night; there might be nonsolar ghosts)
Found: the place where my Las Vegas aunt's house was razed
        (also the place her grandson, my age, has built a new home)
        (does he remember I looked on his test in first grade to spell
        our name?)
Found: the remains from last year's Rez elementary school garden
        (where the current kids learn not just how to name the three sisters)
        (they now know how to grow them together, corn, beans,
        and squash)

Found: the reservoir, that sits on the western end of the reservation
        (the land is only leased to the state, in theory still in the Nation)
        (but anyone with eyes knows they are never tearing it down)

The Lost and Found here are around 50/50, and we're thankful for the ratio.

11.

It is raining so the earth has turned mostly to mud, and I
think of what the minister said when my brother died: "The rain
comes and washes away his prints, so we can move on." I wished
for drought instead, so we wouldn't lose every trace, but it rained
for a week straight, and despite it being April, three feet of snow
landed to make sure the job was done for good.

We visit my mother's grave and, near her resting place,
the grave of that young man who left the way I might have
if I'd had a car that young, and I show you the sculpture
my nephew has welded in his honor to stay with him forever,
a stainless steel lacrosse player, impervious to weather
and heartbreak in ways we'll never know.

We enter my home, a few miles and a million miles away,
and you meet the Bumblebee of my adult life, and he sprinkles
pollen for you, a new voice he has found, mixing paint, heat,
gravity into new shapes, shadows, galaxies, and with your
impossibly generous heart, you give me the real pages
you unlocked my universe with, all those years ago.

12.

Over a few short panels, you tell an infinite story, about love
and hoping and the unendurable waiting for a loved one's letter.

We've waited for the mail, we've told ourselves that letter
has been Lost in the Mail, and maybe it will be Found
in the Mail, sometime, because we don't want to know
the truth because we already know the truth. We know
we always survive the truth, but we know some small part
does not receive the amber protection. That part is lost
to scars we dig into, and rearrange into art, and send that part
back out, to unknowable places, sing to unfamiliar ears.

We hope that whoever needs the message the most, will discover
it where it waits for them. We tell our stories in perpetuity. Patiently
we Test for Echo, waiting for a pingback among the Lost and Found.

On New Year's Eve, My Sister Sends Me a Photo

1.

Most photos that used to be in the Red Album
are gone or damaged beyond desire to keep them.
When fire claimed our history that not even Carlisle
could steal, we crawled through rubble, ignoring
firemen warnings of falling debris and hidden embers.
We found loose stacks, many burned beyond recognition,
and peel them apart. What fire didn't destroy, hoses
dissolved. Our photos grew as hazy as memories.

2.

Is it better to see damaged photos, faces blackened and
smeared beyond recognition or better to keep the original
image stored inside your heart, where maybe you can soften
edges if you want to, improve the light or perhaps just your
smile, make your hair less warped, erase whatever you don't
like about the past with the Photoshop of your mind?

3.

Because I can afford a fancy reproduction now, I talk my brother
into putting on the old Bat-Helmet and we pose together,
two Batmans, short of a Robin. A photo we had, him making
fun of me by wearing the Helmet, my Bat-Belt, and a bath towel
tucked into the collar of a Rolling Stones T-shirt, is gone
for good to flame and smoke, and ash and wind.

4.

After all this time, my family accepts that I will
always be odd man out. I waste money finding
toys I had when we all lived together, when I was

the right age to still love toys. I reconstruct a past
that I often wanted to leave, and reconstruct
a past burned to coals one May afternoon.

They pretend it isn't that weird for a man
to wear a Batman leather jacket and they're
maybe just relieved I don't put on the cowl
for too many people (that they know of).

No matter what sequence of words I write, no
matter what images I reimagine, I wonder if
they will ever understand this is not just an act
of celebration but a declaration of survival.

We are still here, despite everything that has
been taken away any moment we aren't looking.

5.

Sometimes they say yes they understand by
passing along something they know will wind
up in one of the monuments I have spent my
lifetime imperfectly erecting. If I could
rebuild our Dog Street house, who would
live there, knowing it wasn't really the same,
but another inaccurate portrait from my past,
where I have decided which harsh edge to soften,
which memory to exhume and massage?

6.

As the New Year arrives, my sister sends me
a black-and-white aerial shot, maybe taken
in a helicopter or a crop duster, of our house.

The surrounding woods are sparse, full of walking
paths to neighbors, our epic lawn more barren, giant
trees just a hint on the horizon. But this photo is so old,
the "porch," a freezing front room we all endured for
phone privacy in high school, has not yet been built. It
was my grandmother's gift to herself, with the fleeting
money she received for land flooded inside the reservoir.
She wanted something permanent to show for her losses,
but of course, she could not imagine our fire those years later.

7.

I've never seen our home from the air, so tiny
and insignificant on the landscape, it would seem
like a circus clown car if we all left it at one time.
This feels like an out-of-body experience, the kind
people get when they've come close to death and
somehow made their way back to tell of the trip.

Maybe this is what each member of my family witnessed
as they made their way on the Celestial path. Maybe such
a sight made it easier to force my siblings and me to become
elders long before we were ready to take that responsibility
on, long before we were ready to say our goodbyes.

Though the house has been gone so long only the lawn remains
as proof it was there, maybe this is what we'll see when we
leave this place for Skyworld, and Get Back one last time.

.

(Bat-man) Rick - age 2
This picture was taken in the fall.
but I just had the films developed.

Oct- 1967

Liner Notes

Back when albums were strictly physical objects, part of the excitement was the back cover Liner Notes, discussing the production. If you don't like such things, feel free to stop reading now. Sometimes an idea takes a long time to evolve. My first book of poems and paintings used the image of the Indian Head Nickel. The engraving artist combined stereotypically indigenous features from four different men to create one face that he thought was "Indian enough." This may seem irrelevant to you . . . unless you are an indigenous person living right now. All American Indians I know have been told, numerous times, that they "don't look Indian," by someone who doesn't know any indigenous people. We don't fit into the imagination of U.S. culture. Around the same time I was considering this phenomenon, I was studying the shifting visual history of the Beatles throughout their careers. Many fans felt betrayed by this change. These two ideas collided and became something new.

I thought this collision might be an interesting way to explore representation, overlaying iconic images of the Beatles, with those four indigenous men who vanished when they each became one fourth of the Indian Head Nickel portrait. I eventually noted that the Beatles' looks separated most when they started their own record label: Apple. This development seemed like the perfect starting point. That word, that object, led me directly back to Indian identity and all of its complexities.

As you've seen throughout this book, in a lot of American Indian communities, the word "apple" is a derogatory term, meaning "red on the outside, white on the inside." It's reserved for Indians who've learned to effectively "act white when necessary." Yet, in most Indian communities, English is the dominant language, Levi's are worn more often than leggings, and the drums I've heard often originate in digital hip-hop beats instead of traditional water drums. Perhaps the distinction is a matter of degrees. I've learned what it takes to be conversant in the

United States, even as my social dance moves grow rustier and rustier. But peeling a human skin is not nearly as easy as some might believe. Leaving home, though, was something I understood I was going to have to do. After high school, my life was taking me in different directions.

I'd always loved the simple graphic on the Beatles' Apple album labels, and have a few shirts with this emblem. I suspect some people from the Rez have thought: "There's truth in advertising." For some places in our lives, we feel love and dismay in equal measure, and the reservation road I grew up on is such a place. The road's official name is Mount Hope, but as you know by now, most people call it Dog Street. One of my nephews calls himself Dog Street Refugee—a name I wish I had thought up. Most of my siblings live on the reservation, and I live a few minutes away, as I have since college, eternal Dog Street Refugee. Whenever I think of Dog Street, I almost always think of Abbey Road, and maybe that was the real key to this work. Sometimes, you just have to own your choices.

SECTION NOTES

"Apple Records" is what the Beatles called their company, but it might also be an accurate label for the stories formed by the nearly four hundred U.S. Government sponsored Indian Boarding Schools whose sole purpose, from the late nineteenth century well into the second half of the twentieth, was to irreparably wipe out any traces of indigenous cultures in its charges. Three of my four grandparents went to Boarding Schools, and their legacy stays with me always. As such, that seemed like the logical place to start.

The first album on Apple Records, formally, is called *The Beatles*. Most people refer to it as "The White Album," which I couldn't quite see using for the second section. I modified the name to "The Red Album," which also refers to the collection of photos that inspired large parts of it. Endlessly people have claimed the Beatles' White Album is the beginning of the end, four individual musicians with talented sidemen. The poems in this section are about reservation life, in my large extended family, with the shadow of popular culture coloring the observations. We lost most of our family photos from our real Red Album when our original family home, begun in the nineteenth century, burned to the ground in a freak accident in 1994. Of the photos that survive, most were damaged by the fire and the water used to put the fire out. A handful are intact because our mother had given us each some when we moved out. Some of these surviving photos appear in these pages.

Let It Be is considered by a lot of people to be a posthumous album, assembled with a different producer's ear. It began as a project called *Get Back*, an attempt to get back to their roots. Instead it showed how gaps between them had grown wider. The poems in this section examine an irretrievable past through familiar threads, intimate connection, and popular culture.

Abbey Road, the piece between, was the Beatles' last attempt to exist in that one identity before transforming into something else. They've said the cover and title of *Abbey Road* were almost inadvertent, because of production deadlines. Yet it was named after the place where they'd truly become a group, the place they'd recorded most of their work. The album was a map to their end. They chose to conclude their business neatly, rather than with the chaos of *Let It Be*. For *Abbey Road*, they wanted to leave a meaningful document, even taking up most of the second side with a "suite" of unfinished songs, edited together, a gestalt, a whole, more than the sum of its parts. Why did they cross Abbey Road?

I'm well versed in the act of taking last fragments of one identity before leaving it for another, losing the old one forever. "Dog Street," the centerpiece, documents the change, stretching from the time I graduated from high school to the time when I knew I would not return to the reservation, a span a little over a year. This is about the amount of time the Beatles took to discover they were no longer the Beatles and set about crossing that road.

The poems here also reflect my earliest interest in poetry. The poems I wrote through high school were complex rhyming affairs, derived heavily from Pink Floyd's *The Wall*. The more I read contemporary poetry, the more I moved to free verse. These poems represent that migration, divided into rhyming and non-rhyming passages. Each poem is named for the same song in the running order of *Abbey Road*, and each italicized section was composed using the exact syllable, line break, and rhyme scheme of its corresponding song.

A FINAL NOTE ABOUT THE ART

Since this project started as an idea for a series of paintings, I felt strongly that they needed to be included. If you're interested, you can see what they look like, in color and without edits, on my website, <u>www.ericgansworth.com</u>, under the visual art gallery tab for this book.

Much of my visual work from 2000 on, has been a mash-up of popular culture and images taken from the Haudenosaunee, the group of indigenous nations where I am enrolled. My paintings often borrow images from our traditional wampum belts, objects made with purple and white shell beads that document our cultures, ceremonies, history, cosmology, and legal transactions, including treaties among ourselves and with the United States. You can learn detailed information about the wampum belts easily online.

Because the sections of this book called "Apple Records" and "The Red Album" had no real-world album cover analogues, I needed something else. I liked that "records" and "album" could refer to both music and collections of written documents. The section header paintings here are parallel halves of the same painting. The background features a ceremonial wampum belt, flanked by two copies of a western style crest. The wampum is the Tadodaho belt, which focuses on sweeping away sadness and troublesome outside influences, for clear thoughts in council. The crest is from Carlisle, designed by those young Indians conscripted there, to learn a trade—in this case, printing. It is the letter C, surrounded by shapes that seem vaguely "Indian." The book cover font was also designed at Carlisle, for periodicals called *The Red Man* and *The Indian Helper*, meant to promote the successes of life at Carlisle. The apples in each of these cases are no longer whole, but their damaged parts are nearby.

The collage painting interspersed throughout "The Red Album" borrows its organization from the Richard Hamilton poster included in "The White Album," which was created from informal photos provided by each Beatle. This painting uses that collage shape, but the images are taken from my family photos.

The "Dog Street" images obviously mimic the front and back cover of *Abbey Road*, with each Beatle being replaced by self-portraits (surrounded by the inevitable dogs of Dog Street) during the rapid transition period from adolescent to young adult to new adult to adult. Also included are parodies of the Beatles' Apple Records label, sliced open or devoured to explore the lives inside the red skin.

The last painting represents the initial visual idea for *Let It Be*, under its original title, *Get Back*. During the planning stages, the Beatles recreated the cover photo from their first album, *Please Please Me*, looking over a balcony at EMI headquarters. I swapped the Beatles out for members of my family. From left to right are my grandfather, father, oldest brother, and me. My oldest brother was already an adult, heading to Vietnam, when I was born. We are virtually members of different generations, so from that point of view, this represents four generations of my family. I have also added a key wampum belt, the Everlasting Tree, which celebrates survival and cultural continuity, onto the balcony walls heading toward the sky.

Acknowledgments

As always, thank you first and foremost to Larry Plant, first reader, endless reader, root of the tree, believer no matter how preposterous the idea. Thank you to E.R. Baxter III who gave feedback on some early passages I was most concerned about. Nyah-wheh, eternal, to Diversity Jedi charter members Debbie Reese (Nambe Pueblo) and Cynthia Leitich Smith (Muscogee Creek) for their passion. A snapping side-eyes thanks to the people who told me this was a dumb idea, forcing me to ask myself if I were really prepared to pursue the project to its logical end.

A *huge* thank you to Nick Thomas and Arthur A. Levine, first for not rejecting the idea of a poetry book for a younger audience and second, for revisiting the idea, enthusiastically nurturing it in its most fragile state, and seeing it through to the end. Thanks to Jim McCarthy for his wealth of experience and keen sense of detail during a big unexpected change in direction.

Grateful acknowledgement to the following places where some poems were published before, sometimes in earlier forms: *Poetry, NYQ: The New York Quarterly, Native Literatures, Stone Canoe, Ownership, Many Mountains Moving, Superstition Review, Sentence,* and *American Indian Quarterly.* Thank you to Canisius College, specifically the Joseph S. Lowery Estate for Funding Faculty Fellowship in Creative Writing. Thank you also to my colleagues and students who always keep matters of earnestness and craft at the forefront.

Nyah-wheh to Bryan Printup and Rene Rickard of the Tuscarora Environmental Office for generously providing the key photo of my family home from a view I'd never seen. Acknowledgment also to the Cumberland County Historical Society for explicitly identifying the necessary fees, so I could include here their photo of my grandfather from his time in The Carlisle Indian School. Their volume, *The Indian*

Industrial School, was the first place I encountered this photo. This book also has special meaning for me, as it led to my friendship with Debbie Reese. Debbie knew I was looking for a copy, and thoughtfully gave me hers, the first day we met in person.

Some years, I see extended family mostly at funerals, a typical sad state of affairs once you become the Elder Generation. At one this past summer, a cousin asked if my next book was going to be about our family again. I said yes, and she laughed, observing I was lucky to have been born into such an interesting family. I couldn't agree more. Nyah-wheh to my family, complex, fascinating, and inspiring, even when they don't know it.

About the Author

Eric Gansworth S·ha-weñ na-sae? is Lowery Writer-in-Residence and Professor of English at Canisius College in Buffalo, NY, and was recently NEH Distinguished Visiting Professor at Colgate University. An enrolled Onondaga, he was born and raised at the Tuscarora Nation. He is the author of ten books; his first for young adults, *If I Ever Get Out of Here*, was a YALSA Best Fiction for Young Adults pick and an American Indian Library Association Young Adult Honor selection. His second, *Give Me Some Truth*, was an NPR, *Boston Globe*, and *School Library Journal* Best Book of the Year. His books for adults include *Extra Indians* (American Book Award, NAIBA Book of the Year), *Mending Skins* (PEN Oakland Award) and *A Half-Life of Cardio-Pulmonary Function*, (National Book Critics Circle's "Good Reads List" for Spring 2008). Just Buffalo Literary Center and its partners recently selected him for inclusion in *Lit City*, a public arts project celebrating Buffalo's literary legacy.

Gansworth is also a visual artist, and generally incorporates paintings as integral elements into his written work. His first full length dramatic work, *Re-Creation Story*, was part of the Public Theater's Native Theater Festival, in NYC. His work has been widely shown and anthologized and has appeared in *Iroquois Art, Power, and History*; *Poetry*; *The Kenyon Review*; *Shenandoah*; *The Boston Review*; *Third Coast*; and *The Yellow Medicine Review*; among other places.

Some Notes on this Book's Production

The art for the jacket was created digitally by Filip Peraić using Adobe Illustrator. The art for the interiors was created by Eric Gansworth using gouache on 140-lb. 100% cotton Arches Cold Pressed Watercolor Paper blocks and family photo references, salvaged from fire and donated by family. The photographs were gathered from various sources by Eric Gansworth. The text was set by Semadar Megged in Electra, a serif typeface originally designed by William Addison Dwiggins, released through Linotype in 1935 and intended to be a "modern roman type letter" with "personality". The display was set in Agency FB, a sans-serif typeface designed by David Berlow in 1995 for Font Bureau, building off of titling face designs by Morris Fuller Benton in the 1930s. The book was printed on FSC™-certified 98gsm Yunshidai Ivory paper and bound in China.

Production was supervised by Leslie Cohen and Freesia Blizard
Book interiors designed by Semadar Megged
Edited by Nick Thomas

LEVINE QUERIDO